The Wonderful World
of
Ladybird Books
for Grown-Ups

The Wonderful World
of
Ladybird Books
for Grown-Ups

Jason Hazeley & Joel Morris

MICHAEL JOSEPH
UK | USA | Canada | Ireland | Australia
India | New Zealand | South Africa

Michael Joseph is part of the Penguin Random House group of companies whose
addresses can be found at global.penguinrandomhouse.com

First published 2018
001

Book design by Alex Morris

Printed in Italy by L.E.G.O. S.p.A

A CIP catalogue record for this book is available from the British Library

ISBN: 978–0–241–36404–8

www.greenpenguin.co.uk

Penguin Random House is committed to a
sustainable future for our business, our readers
and our planet. This book is made from Forest
Stewardship Council© certified paper.

For Helen & Jenny
and
Ronnie & Rowland

a complete
list of
the new
Ladybirds
For
Grown–Ups

all titles 15p

Contents

They're not for you...

Children love the bright colours and clear writing of Ladybird Books.

But so do grown–ups.

With their colourful illustrations, carefully chosen words, and thoughtful matching of text and picture, Ladybird Books for Grown–Ups make the hard parts of being a grown–up that little bit easier.

And whether you're getting a mortgage or a replacement hip, the Ladybird series is here to help.

So when you visit your local book shop, make sure you look on the right shelf.

And tell your children they've got Ladybirds of their own.

Ladybird Books for
GROWN–UPS

Introduction

Everyone knows that being a grown-up is a difficult stage of life. The world can seem such a confusing place. There are so many things to learn. What is an offset mortgage? Why have I heard of no-one playing at Wimbledon this year? What are chia seeds for? Is this actually music? Can I wash these new bank notes? What is a break-out space? When did one of my hips start clicking? Why are phones getting bigger again? Will I ever get round to reading that book I've had for ten years but never opened? Isn't a washing-up bowl just a sink within a sink? Who are these people on TV and why are they only famous for being on TV? When did lorries start talking? Why can't I use a password I've used before? Can anyone understand how to work the air conditioning? What's the difference between a meeting and a pre-meeting? How long does it take to shape that beard in the morning? Who reads the terms and conditions? Who writes them? What do vegans feed their pet dogs? Where did fugly words like 'mentertainment,' 'mantiques' and 'fugly' come from? Why did I ever go camping? Will I have to cave in and increase the font size on my phone? What if the happiest moment of my life has already happened?

The *Ladybird Books For Grown-Ups* were specially planned to help grown-ups with the world about them.

This book is a celebration of those books, which have come to take a very special place in the broken hearts, tired minds and downstairs toilets of grown-ups everywhere.

Fun & Games

Fun & Games

Grown-ups love to enjoy themselves. Whether it's changing the washer on a garden tap in the middle of a cold snap or queueing for forty-five minutes in a bank because there are still people who inexplicably write cheques, there is so much for a grown-up to enjoy.

There are forms to fill in, tyres to pump up, emails to answer, washing-up to be put away, operating systems to update, things to take to the dump, parking fines to pay, hospital appointments to keep, gutters to clear, premiums to renew, chuggers to talk to, lunch breaks to work through, deliveries to wait in for, statins to remember to take, road closures to negotiate, teambuilding exercises to enjoy, panic attacks to have and wills to write.

Being a grown-up means there's always plenty to do.

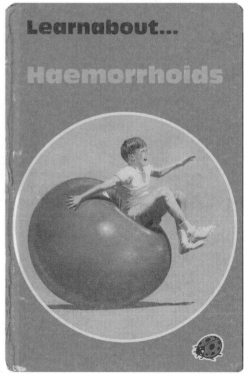

HOPKINS' TEAM ~ BUILDING WEEK ~ END

A Lady-bird Book

"Where is Hopkins?" worries Simons,
  The session is about to start.
"He will miss the improv workshop,
  That usually is my favourite part."

Mallinson and Daniels find him,
  Slumped beneath a shady oak,
"He is not used to lunchtime drinking,"
  Says Daniels, who has stuck to Coke.

The very first *Ladybird Book For Grown-Ups* – like every one since – was folded and cut from a single sheet of paper, making it the perfect size for grown-up hands, and easily slipped into a suit pocket or briefcase. The first book told the tale of a little rabbit who learns that his bar receipts for a teambuilding weekend can be written off against tax under 'entertaining', with terrible consequences. The Hopkins books were written in verse, but proved enormously popular.

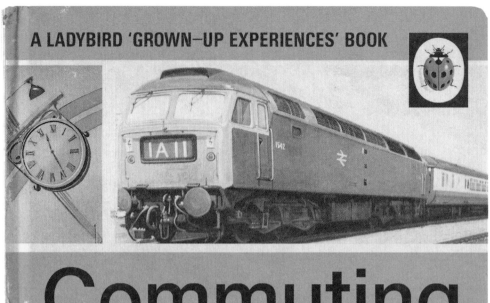

A LADYBIRD 'GROWN—UP EXPERIENCES' BOOK

Commuting

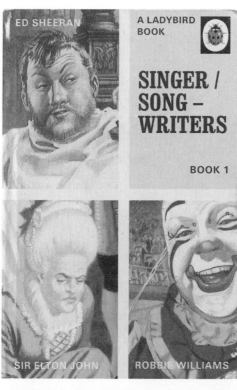

ED SHEERAN

A LADYBIRD BOOK

SINGER / SONG – WRITERS

BOOK 1

SIR ELTON JOHN   ROBBIE WILLIAMS

'WELL—LOVED TALES'

The Great Escape

A LADYBIRD BOOK FOR GROWN-UPS

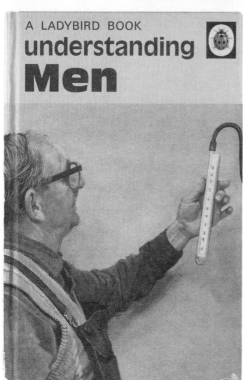

A LADYBIRD BOOK

understanding Men

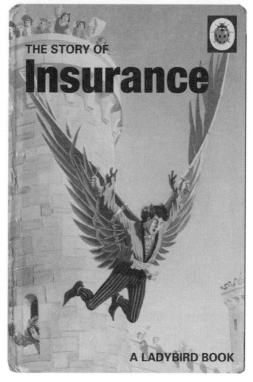

THE STORY OF

Insurance

A LADYBIRD BOOK

The *Well-Loved Tales* series included many stories popular with grown-ups, such as this one about Margo's wind-break falling over.

'WELL—LOVED TALES'

The Good Life

A LADYBIRD BOOK FOR GROWN-UPS

Learnabout...
Michael Palin

THE STORY OF
FIGHTS
A LADYBIRD 'DUBIOUS ACHIEVEMENTS' BOOK

THE LADYBIRD BOOK OF

THE VEGAN

'Places We Go'

THE BENEFITS OFFICE

A LADYBIRD BOOK FOR GROWN–UPS

The original artwork for *Moving House* was lost when the publisher relocated.

A LADYBIRD 'Modern Irritations' Book

MOVING HOUSE

S.L. LOW REMOVALS

"What you're paying for here, really," says the estate agent, "is the location."

Ginny has vacuum—cleaned, put on some classical music, and baked bread. She has made some fresh coffee. Everything smells and looks and sounds great.

The buyers want garden access. Ginny's flat does not have garden access.

Next time, Ginny thinks, she will remember to make her flat smell of garden access.

Anthiny has been waiting six weeks for the local council to issue the sales memos and contracts to one of the buyers in his chain.

On Saturday, he was informed they have not started the process and will not say why.

Anthiny is glad to be back at work today. It takes his mind off the stress of house–buying.

16

Bob is a conveyancing solicitor. He has been helping people move house for 35 years, which means Bob never worries or hurries.

Bob does not have an e–mail address. Sometimes he does not answer his phone. Today he is printing some urgent documents on a hot metal press which he will send by second class post.

"The old ways are the best," says Bob.

20

"They're new-builds," says the estate agent, "so you will get all your amenities, your wi-fi, your water meter, all there already for when you move in."

"It's quite small," says Megan.

"Wi-fi. Everything," says the estate agent.

Well-Loved Tales: *Raiders of The Lost Ark* was later made into a film.

The archaeologist ran around. He looked everywhere. Behind the fruit carts. Under the tables. But he could not see the lady.

Then he heard a shout... in a lady's voice. He looked around. The lady was in a basket. The bad foreigners were taking her away.

He pulled out his gun. He might need to shoot somebody. "And quickly," he thought, "because I really need the toilet."

Everybody was digging. The bad foreigners were digging in one place. And the archaeologist and his friends the good foreigners were digging in another.

"Dig faster," the archaeologist said to the good foreigners. But he did not dig. He was very busy adjusting his hat.

From *Well-Loved Tales: Raiders of The Lost Ark.*

BELOW
'"Our prize is awaited in Berlin," said the Frenchman.'

"Snakes," said the archaeologist. "Why did it have to be snakes?"

The archaeologist's friend knew that the archaeologist was especially scared of snakes.

"You go first," said the friend.

He was not a very good friend.

32

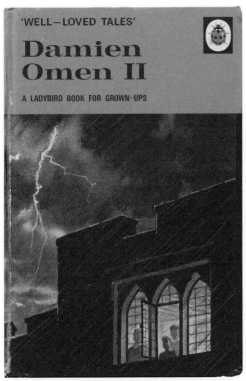

'WELL—LOVED TALES'

Damien Omen II

A LADYBIRD BOOK FOR GROWN-UPS

PLACES TO LEAVE THEM

Someone's Birthday

A LADYBIRD BOOK FOR GROWN-UPS

BOTTOM LEFT
Lord Sugar has publicly credited his success to having been given a copy of *How To Make A Million Pounds* at a young age, and selling it at a profit.

how to make A Million Pounds

THE LADYBIRD BOOK OF

COMPLAINING ABOUT THE BBC

THE LADYBIRD BOOK OF

THE BEST MAN

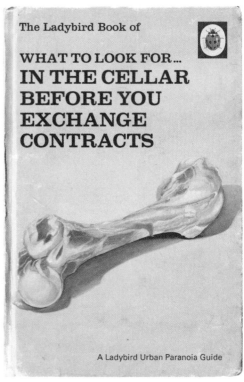

The Ladybird Book of

WHAT TO LOOK FOR... IN THE CELLAR BEFORE YOU EXCHANGE CONTRACTS

A Ladybird Urban Paranoia Guide

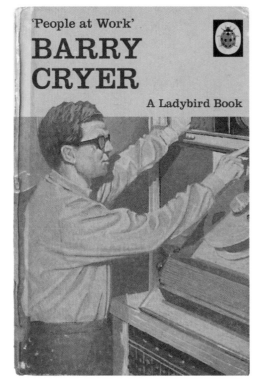

'People at Work'

BARRY CRYER

A Ladybird Book

A LADYBIRD BOOK

understanding Croydon

'Robots Who Work For Us'

THE CYBORG

A LADYBIRD BOOK

This was the only title in the *Robots Who Work For Us* series that was published. Others on Metal Mickey and Sergeant Bash from Robot Wars never made it to print.

Grown-ups never stop learning

Your customers know what they want.

But if you're in the know, you'll know that they also know what they don't know.

And we know that you know that if they want to know what they don't know, you'll know where to go...

To a Ladybird.

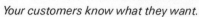

LADYBIRD BOOKS FOR GROWN–UPS
Because you never know what you'll need to know.

2/6

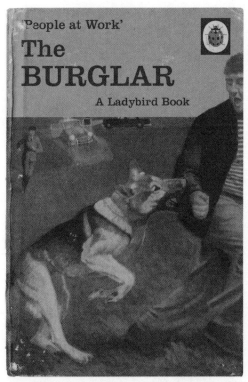

'People at Work'
The
BURGLAR
A Ladybird Book

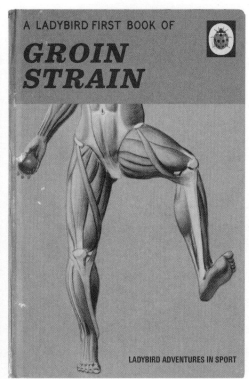

A LADYBIRD FIRST BOOK OF
GROIN
STRAIN
LADYBIRD ADVENTURES IN SPORT

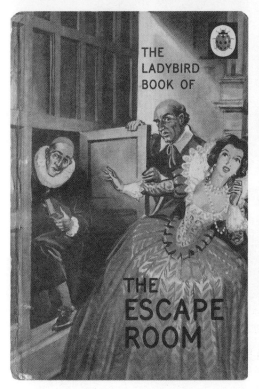

THE
LADYBIRD
BOOK OF

THE
ESCAPE
ROOM

78c
We don't
any more
The Ladybird Key Words
Scheme For Grown-Ups

Adventure

Adventure

Being a grown-up is such an adventure. One minute you are up for promotion and looking for a new house with your partner, the next the company is relocating to Holland, you're having to take a mortgage holiday, and your relationship is on the rocks.

And there are so many exciting places to explore: crowded airports, windowless meeting rooms, overstretched doctors' surgeries, motorway service station toilets, the bathroom fittings aisle of B&Q, retirement homes that vaguely smell of milk, solicitor's offices above charity shops, budget hotels in converted office blocks miles from anywhere to buy food or drink, fading small towns where the crime rate has gone up – it's a world full of adventure for a grown-up.

And you never know what's round the next corner.

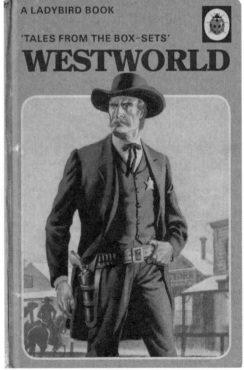

The author of *People At Work: The Ninja*, T.D. Mandrape was a part-time ninja who had worked for the Guernsey police department and David Essex.

'People at Work'

The NINJA

A Ladybird Book

A LADYBIRD BOOK

understanding **Punk**

63f **They never listen**

The Ladybird Key Words Scheme For Grown–Ups

TOP LEFT
Understanding Punk was banned by Buckinghamshire Libraries for encouraging spitting in the non-fiction section.

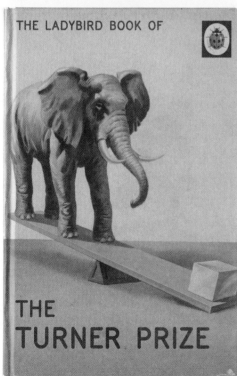

THE LADYBIRD BOOK OF

THE TURNER PRIZE

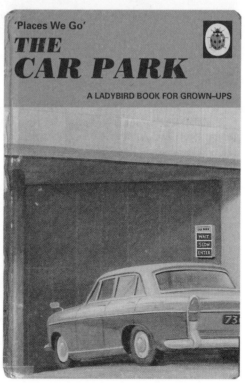

'Places We Go'

THE CAR PARK

A LADYBIRD BOOK FOR GROWN–UPS

Well-Loved Tales: The Spy Who Loved Me is fondly remembered by adventurous boys and girls of all ages, and was adapted for *Ladybird Books For Grown-Ups* by G. E. R. Wall, in his distinctive style. Wall was well-known for his work on manuals for Bendix kettles.

'WELL—LOVED TALES'

The Spy Who Loved Me

A LADYBIRD BOOK FOR GROWN-UPS

The Secret Agent drove his car as fast as he could, but he could not get away from the helicopter.

Bang! Boom! Bang! Boom! Bombs exploded on the road. The Helicopter Lady smiled. She knew that the road ended in a very big drop.

The Secret Agent pushed a button. "This car has a special surprise," he thought, and he smiled too.

2

The Secret Agent skied as fast as he could, but he could not get away from the Evil Skier.

Bang! Boom! Bang! Boom! Bombs exploded in the snow. The Evil Skier smiled. He knew that the ski–slope ended in a very big drop.

The Secret Agent pushed a button. "These ski–poles have a special surprise," he thought, and he smiled too.

8

The much-anticipated *Moonraker* was another big hit for adapter G. E. R. Wall. Years later, Wall discovered a family connection with the film franchise: producer Cubby Broccoli's ancestors had invented one of the vegetables that his own father grew in his allotment.

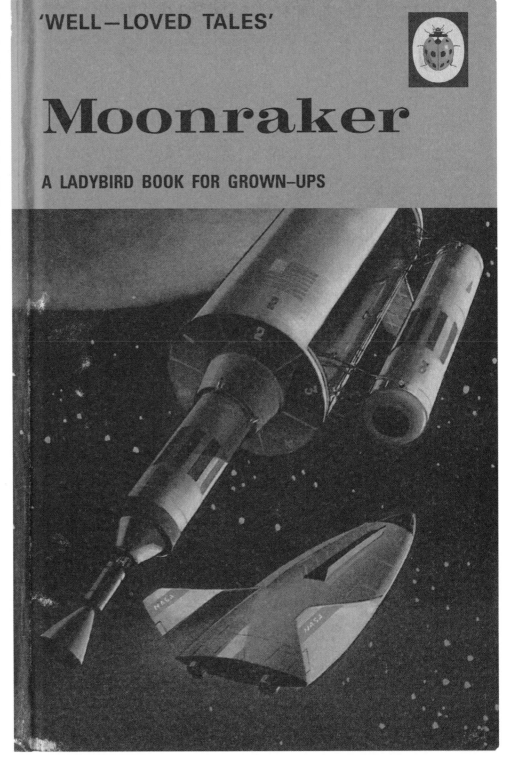

'WELL—LOVED TALES'

Moonraker

A LADYBIRD BOOK FOR GROWN—UPS

The Secret Agent drove his boat as fast as he could, but he could not get away from the Giant.

Splash! Boom! Splash! Boom! Bombs exploded in the water. The Giant smiled. He knew that the river ended in a very big drop.

The Secret Agent pushed a button. "This boat has a special surprise," he thought, and he smiled too.

The Secret Agent drove his gondola as fast as he could, but he could not get away from the Evil Gondolier.

Splash! Splash! Splash! Splash! Knives landed in the canal. The Evil Gondolier smiled. He knew that the canal ended in a famously closed square.

The Secret Agent pushed a button. "This gondola has a special surprise," he thought, and a pigeon looked at him, twice.

All titles in the *Well-Loved Tales: Series 007* were written by G. E. R. Wall, with the exception of *Octopussy* which was by Kevin Keegan.

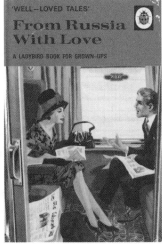

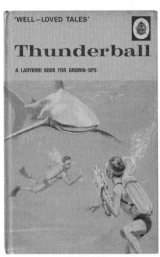

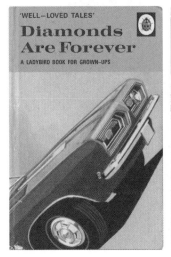

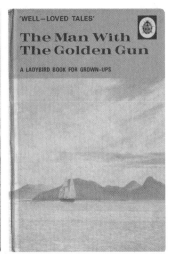

'WELL—LOVED TALES'

For Your Eyes Only

A LADYBIRD BOOK FOR GROWN-UPS

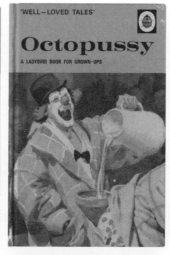

'WELL—LOVED TALES'

Octopussy

A LADYBIRD BOOK FOR GROWN-UPS

'WELL—LOVED TALES'

A View To A Kill

A LADYBIRD BOOK FOR GROWN-UPS

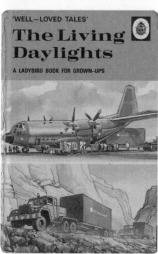

'WELL—LOVED TALES'

The Living Daylights

A LADYBIRD BOOK FOR GROWN-UPS

'WELL—LOVED TALES'

Licence To Kill

A LADYBIRD BOOK FOR GROWN-UPS

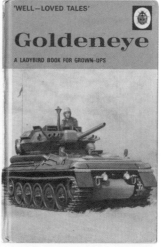

'WELL—LOVED TALES'

Goldeneye

A LADYBIRD BOOK FOR GROWN-UPS

'WELL—LOVED TALES'

Tomorrow Never Dies

A LADYBIRD BOOK FOR GROWN-UPS

'WELL—LOVED TALES'

The World Is Not Enough

A LADYBIRD BOOK FOR GROWN-UPS

'WELL—LOVED TALES'

Die Another Day

A LADYBIRD BOOK FOR GROWN-UPS

'Unwelcome Chores'

EXCHANGING YOUR DETAILS

BOOK 4

A LADYBIRD BOOK

THE LADYBIRD BOOK OF
THE CIVIL
PARTNERSHIP

Booksellers who tried to return unsold copies of *The Ladybird Book of Nightmares* to the publishers would usually find it under their pillow the next morning.

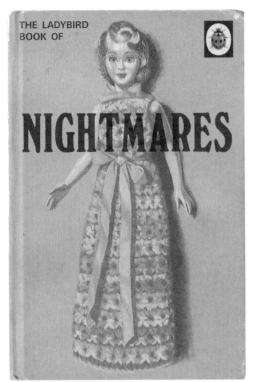

read it your self

Slaughterhouse-Five

reading level 1945

The *Read It Yourself* series enabled grown-ups to pretend they had read books that they simply did not have time to read. This edition was written by the original author.

A Ladybird Child Management Handbook

25 SECRETS OF HIGHLY SUCCESSFUL CARE–GIVERS

Aled has called his son Ivor to a meeting to discuss colourway options for his drawing.

Aled wants Ivor to push back on the green and maximise his teal opportunities. He also questions whether the park is low-hanging fruit in subject matter terms, and if Ivor should refresh his piece.

"I've onboarded your feedback, Daddy," says Ivor. "Let me take this off-line and circle back to you".

18

Best practice in mentoring Hide And Seek finds the effective care-giver making sure their wards operate with maximum contestability.

The seekee should optimise their concealment advantages and ladder in any outlook learnings, while the pursuing party should thought-shower any challenging positional outliers and pipeline them into their gameplan.

30

THE LADYBIRD BOOK OF

Psychedelia

The Ladybird Book of Psychedelia was the only Ladybird Book for Grown-Ups to be issued as a double gatefold edition.

Learnabout...
Ocado

THE LADYBIRD
BOOK OF

HIP—
HOP

TOP RIGHT
The author of *The Ladybird Book of Hip-Hop*, The Rev. D. W. Chipsnorth, wrote no other titles for Ladybird, though he found great success later with his work for Death Row Board Books.

The Car Boot Sale Adventure

48b

Key Words Scheme
for Grown—Ups

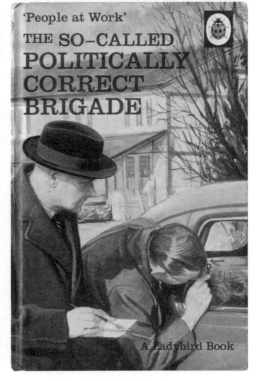

'People at Work'
THE SO—CALLED
**POLITICALLY
CORRECT
BRIGADE**

A Ladybird Book

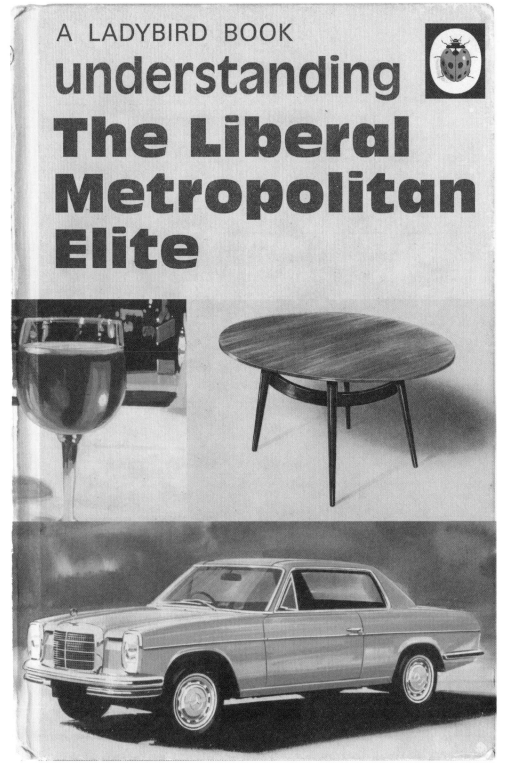

A LADYBIRD BOOK

understanding The Liberal Metropolitan Elite

The school year starts, and Archie has some interesting new friends in his class.

There are twin sisters called Flickr and Superfood and a boy who identifies as a sloth.

The only newspaper on the flight to Biarritz was the Daily Mail, so Ness ended up reading a piece about the so-called liberal left box-ticking gender-quota bien pensants of the minority mob which made her very cross.

"He's made these people up," she fumes to herself.

So she puts the paper in the bin, sips her Seedlip and elderflower pressé with a sugar-snap pea garnish, and goes back to her book on ethno-socialism.

Krzysz would like to celebrate Diwali with his neighbours, but cannot decide whether this would be a charming act of community outreach or a dreadful act of cultural appropriation.

He likes the Chowdhurys and does not want to upset them.

"Maybe I'll just go out for a curry instead," he thinks.

28

Huw saw some amazing things at Glastonbury this year.

Many of them were in his head.

46

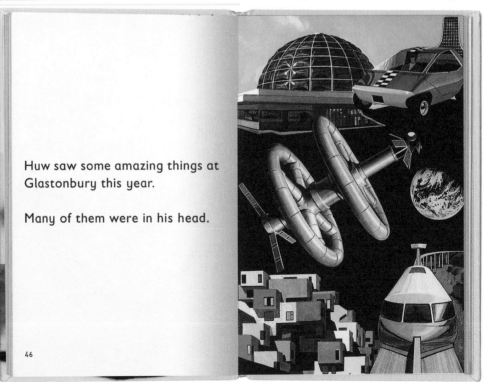

54

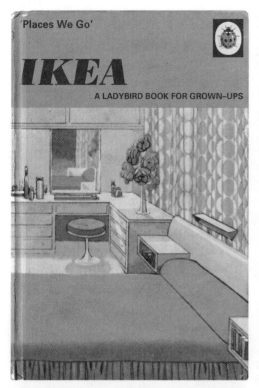

'Places We Go'

IKEA

A LADYBIRD BOOK FOR GROWN–UPS

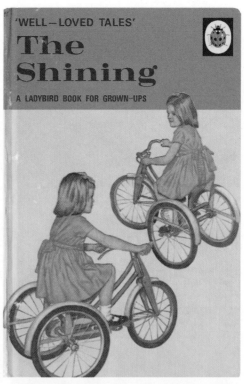

'WELL—LOVED TALES'

The Shining

A LADYBIRD BOOK FOR GROWN–UPS

Places We Go: IKEA was *Ladybird Books For Grown-Ups*'s only self-assembly title. Flat-packing the books enabled 120 to be fitted in each box, rather than the more usual 118.

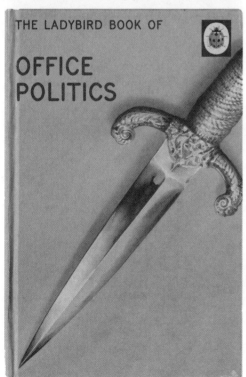

THE LADYBIRD BOOK OF

OFFICE POLITICS

Screen-time is easier

85e

Key Words Scheme for Grown—Ups

The World Around Us

The World Around Us

No matter how big a grown-up you are, the world seems a very big place. There are so many things to see.

Look over there! A plastic bag caught in a tree. And look at that! A man with a megaphone shouting to complete strangers about God. And look! A Ford Focus 1.6 Zetec.

Overseas, things get even more exciting. In Thailand, they have two types of beer. In Italy, they have road tolls. In America, they have slightly different paper sizes.

And the natural world is full of surprises, too. You can eat dogs in the Philippines. You can hunt and kill elephants in South Africa. And, in Australia, there are spiders and fish that can kill you.

What a thrilling world it is for a grown-up.

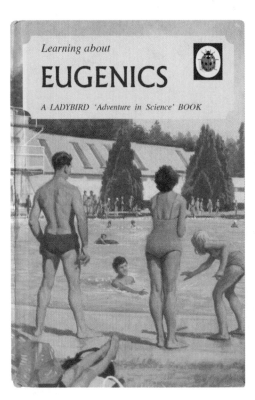

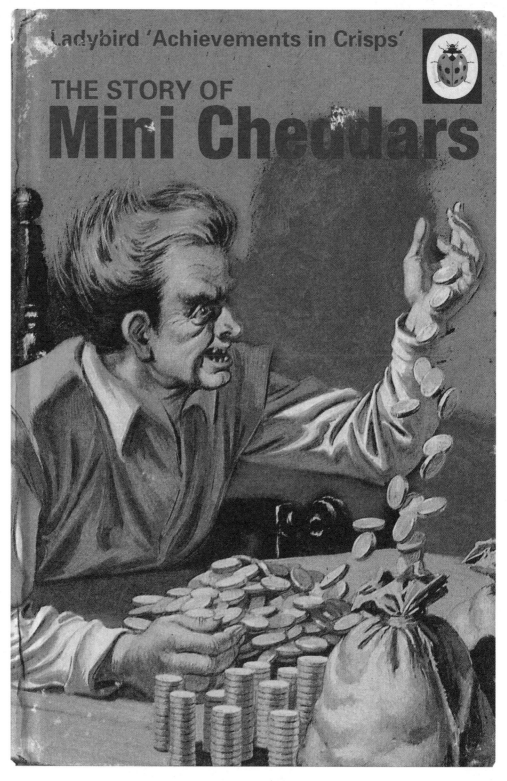

C.T. Nimpnon was the in-house food historian. He also wrote *The Glorious Twiglet* and *The Long Road To Monster Munch*.

Ladybird 'Achievements in Crisps'

THE STORY OF
Mini Cheddars

Sir Hopgood Cheddar

Sir Hopgood Cheddar was one of the nineteenth century's most eminent men of science.

He developed the medical classification of hiccups along the Hopgood Scale that we all still use today, and was knighted by Queen Victoria for his now discredited work with live chickens. But one achievement eluded him: the transformation of cheese into biscuit form.

Crippled by ill–health, Cheddar worked long hours in his laboratory, sleeping under his desk, his fingers yellow and stinking.

6

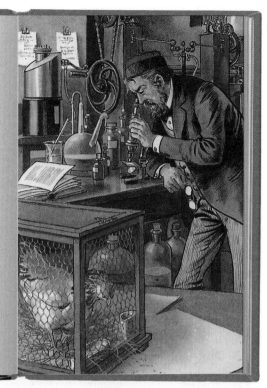

A French disaster

Cheddar's ideas were influenced by the French scientist Le Comte de Croustille, who in 1809 had discovered how to turn gruyere into a crude biscuit disc the size of a dart–board.

De Croustille's experimental 'Fromage–Soleil' was a breakthrough but proved highly unstable. At a presentation to an imperial panel in 1811, one of his prototype cheese discs slipped its moorings and rolled fatally down–hill, crushing Napoleon's personal newsagent.

De Croustille was exiled to the Île de Pompon and abandoned his experiments.

8

From *Ladybird Achievments in Crisps: The Story of Mini Cheddars.*

BELOW
'Pouring the cheese plasma'.

A new dawn for crisps

Cheddar met with the Minister for War at a club in Whitehall. He was to head a top–secret research group with the aim of supplying rations to troops in Crimea. The budget was limitless, but time was of the essence.

Within six months, Cheddar had created a stable cheese biscuit that could be manufactured in bulk and shipped overseas in sealed bags.

He named his invention after his daughter, Minnie, and British soldiers were soon eating hearty perforated cheese snack feasts in the field.

12

62

'Places We Go'
UPSTAIRS
A LADYBIRD BOOK FOR GROWN–UPS

talkabout
networking

BOTTOM LEFT
The Ladybird Book of The By-Pass was an attempt to cash in on the 'Bypassmania' that was sweeping the U.K.

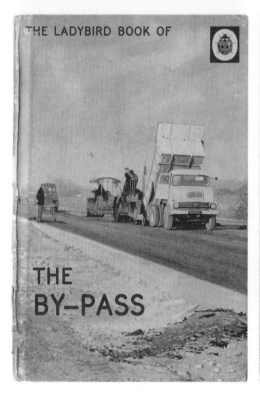

THE LADYBIRD BOOK OF

THE
BY–PASS

A LADYBIRD BOOK
'TALES FROM THE BOX–SETS'
THE HAND-MAID'S TALE

BOTTOM LEFT
The KLF ordered a million copies of *People At Work: The KLF* and set fire to them all for a thing.

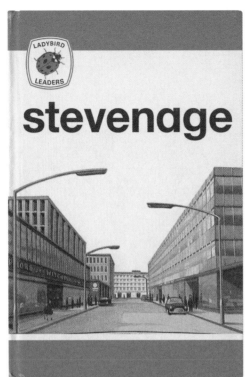

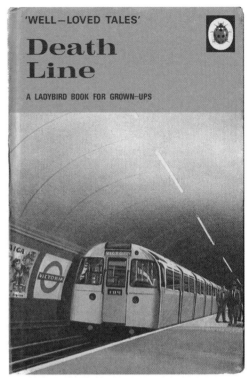

A Ladybird Book

PROBABLY PENGUINS

Birdwatching with Dad

This Ladybird Book was sadly wiped from the archive in a space-saving exercise. Luckily, a copy of some of the illustrations had been made by a fan, using black and white paint, meaning that a restored edition of the entire book could be released three decades later, the story elements approximated using a state-of-the-art combination of guesswork and Wikipedia.

A LADYBIRD 'MISSING BELIEVED WIPED' TALE

The Evil of the Daleks

Jamie stepped out of the mirror cabinet. He had travelled through time, using static electricity, just as the Doctor had said would happen.

He found Victoria. "Come with me," he said. "I am rescuing you."

Jamie and Victoria ran down some corridors together for a while.

But the Daleks were there.

"Exterminate," said the Daleks.

8

"I was promised the secret of alchemy by my friends the Daleks," said Maxtible.

"But now I have something even more precious. I have absorbed The Dalek Factor. I am a hybrid. A human Dalek."

Maxtible laughed for a long time.

"Exterminate," said the Daleks.

8

These books, published as a pair, were very popular in the North and the South. Readers in Scotland had their own book.

'How it works'

THE

NORTHERNER

A LADYBIRD BOOK

'How it works'

THE
SOUTHERNER

A LADYBIRD BOOK

BOTTOM LEFT
The Story of Amazon was a bestseller, despite Amazon's refusal to stock it.

'People at Work'
The BILLIONAIRE
A Ladybird Book

'How it works'
THE PODCASTER

THE STORY OF
AMAZON
A Ladybird Book

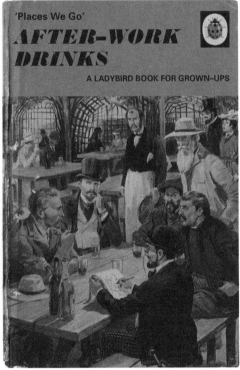

'Places We Go'
AFTER-WORK DRINKS
A LADYBIRD BOOK FOR GROWN-UPS

'People at Work'

The ILLUMINATI

A Ladybird Book

People At Work: The Illuminati was the subject of a federal ban in the U.S.A.

Great Civilisations

THE
MODS

A LADYBIRD BOOK FOR GROWN—UPS

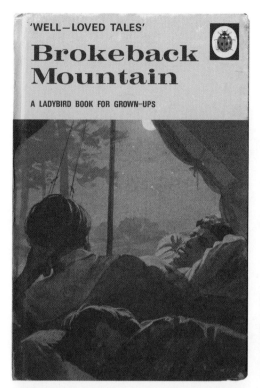

'WELL—LOVED TALES'

Brokeback Mountain

A LADYBIRD BOOK FOR GROWN-UPS

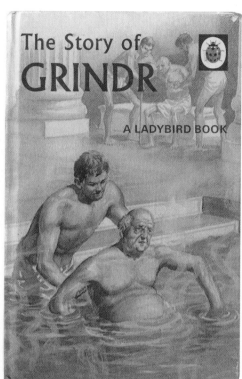

The Story of GRINDR

A LADYBIRD BOOK

BOTTOM RIGHT *Learnabout Parallel Parking* was used by the Co-op Motoring School for many years, along with *Learnabout The Three-Point Turn* and *Learnabout Reversing Round A Corner.*

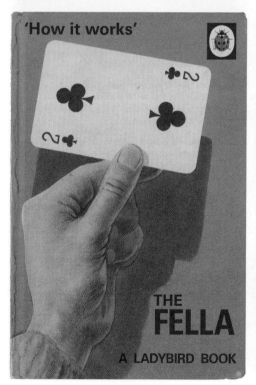

'How it works'

THE FELLA

A LADYBIRD BOOK

Learnabout...
Parallel Parking

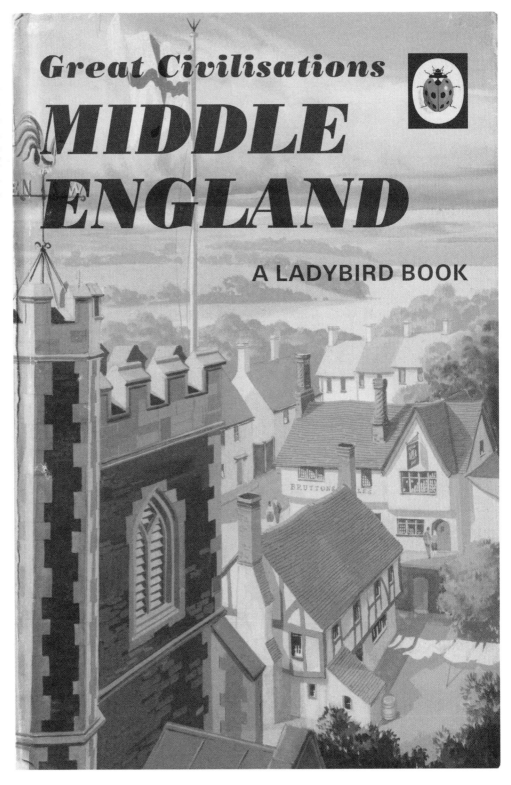

Middle England was the most popular of the *Great Civilisations* series and Quentin Letts called for it to join the Bible and the complete works of Shakespeare as *Desert Island Discs*' third compulsory book.

Great Civilisations

MIDDLE ENGLAND

A LADYBIRD BOOK

Margaret loves her front door.

On one side of Margaret's front door are all the trade unionists, radicals, feminists, social workers, benefits cheats, BBC types, republicans, Turner prizewinners, student layabouts, so—called vegetarians, gender—benders, Italians, community leaders and that Frankie Boyle.

And safely on the other side is Margaret.

8

Newton Hamborough is the first town in England to abandon fossil fuels and power itself entirely on common sense.

18

From *Great Civilisations: Middle England.*

Bernard is thinking about his turnip.

Bernard has been thinking about his turnip all year. He knows his turnip must win the turnip prize at the village turnip festival.

Throwing himself into his turnip has really given him some focus.

He has not thrown himself into anything this much since John Major's cones hotline.

20

Terry has been in London for a day for work.

Terry did not like it. He never does.

But later he will be back home where the air is better and the schools are better and the people are better and everything is better and by the time he gets back, the supermarket is shut and there is no taxi at the station and he has to walk three miles home in mud.

"This," thinks Terry, "is England."

22

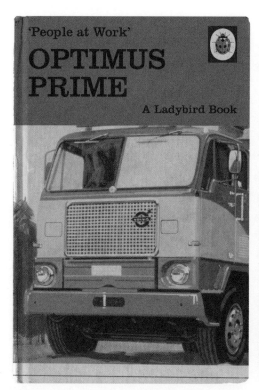

'People at Work'

OPTIMUS PRIME

A Ladybird Book

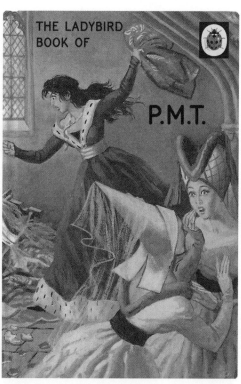

THE LADYBIRD BOOK OF

P.M.T.

A LADYBIRD BOOK

making a punnet of electric raspberries

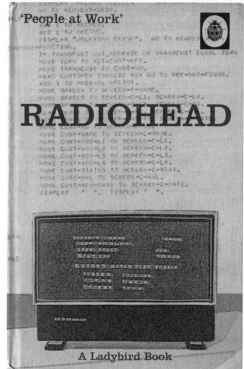

'People at Work'

RADIOHEAD

A Ladybird Book

BOTTOM LEFT
Making A Punnet of Electric Raspberries was withdrawn from sale after its science was called into question by the Royal Institution.

Ladybird Books For Grown-Ups were translated into many foreign languages, such as Scandinavian, European and Cockney.

43j **Bøleg ì Prygt**

21ø **Wìndi windi kjemepløst windi-wìndi**

EN LADENBUG BÜG

Jadg uns...
Im Bolløkstadt!

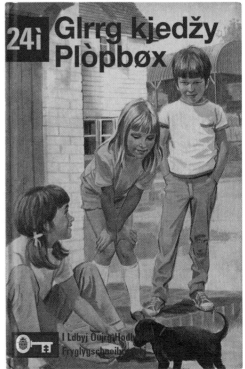

24ì **Glrrg kjedžy Plòpbøx**

'Come funziona'

GLI
SCICCICCICCINI

A LADYBIRD BOOK

bunnyabout
the apples
and pears

29é Jois diçon
'blub-blob'

Plaçon Le Nibu-le-hondelle
fronteux se chataureon

Schnotzig
frühdibum 71f

Wortensitzen für
Die Großobener

The *Ladybird Book of The Ladybird Book* was, according to author N.F. Point, meant to 'bring a touch of Magritte' to the range. It sold very poorly.

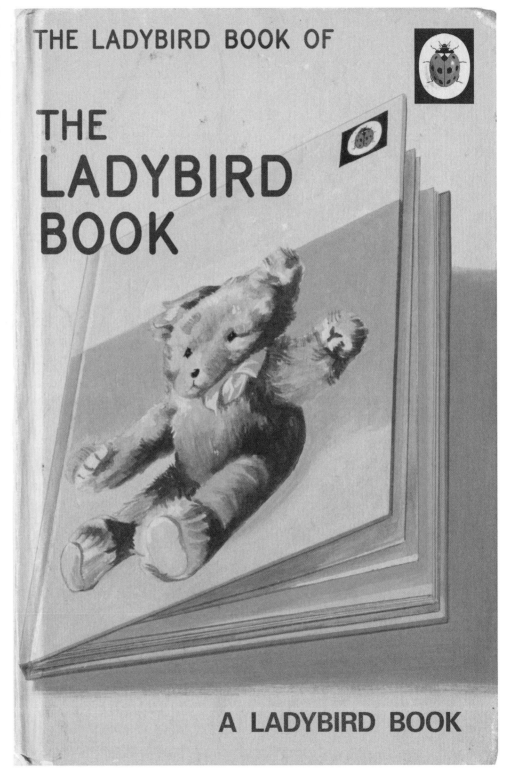

THE LADYBIRD BOOK OF

THE
LADYBIRD
BOOK

A LADYBIRD BOOK

In printing, it costs money to reproduce different images.

These so-called "end-papers" can also be found at the front and back of this book.

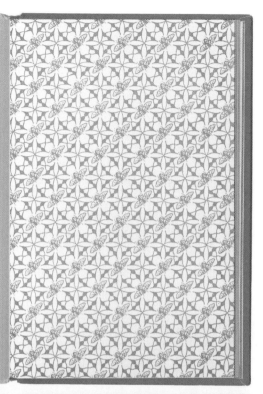

14

This is a picture of the printing press on which this picture of a printing press was printed.

28

Sometimes, books contain small mistakes. But this happens very seldom and they are usually spotted long before the book goes into print.

44

Sometimes, books contain small mistakes. But this happens very seldom and they are usually spotted long before the book goes into print.

44

From The Ladybird Book Of The Ladybird Book.

THE FUTURE IS HERE............
THE FUTURE IS HERE............
THE FUTURE IS HERE

Ladybird Books for Grown-Ups have grown up themselves.

Because the best-selling series is moving into the computers-age, and the results are out-of-this-world.

Welcome Ladybird Books for Grown-Ups...
on Digital 5" Floppy-Disc!

The first eight titles are now available, with the same clear, helpful text that you know and love.

Then, at the click of a space-bar, Ladybird's bright, colourful illustrations... but updated for a new era.

It's possible you might never look at a book again!

LADYBIRD BOOKS
FOR
GROWN-UPS

At Work

At Work

All grown-ups like to work. Work can be fun, and you get paid for it too.

But most people do exciting jobs which make them very happy: things like being a bailiff, working in a meat-packing factory, or sitting in front of those green metal boxes on street corners and rearranging all the brightly coloured wires inside them.

If grown-ups did not work, they would have no money to spend on grown-up things that they like, such as railway season tickets and professional liability insurance and accountancy fees and smart suits and tools for work, and petrol for commuting and leaving gifts for colleagues and superfast broadband for the home office and after-school clubs and daytime childcare.

If grown-ups work ever so hard, and ask nicely for the time off, they may even be able to do something fun outside work, like take a relaxing holiday. There's no better way to get back some energy and leave them raring to go... to work!

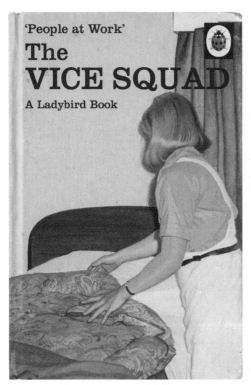

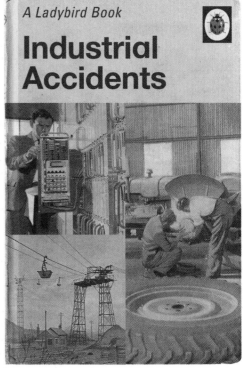

This was intended to be one of a series on great actors, but the second title in the series, *The Story of Vin Diesel*, was withdrawn following a legal dispute.

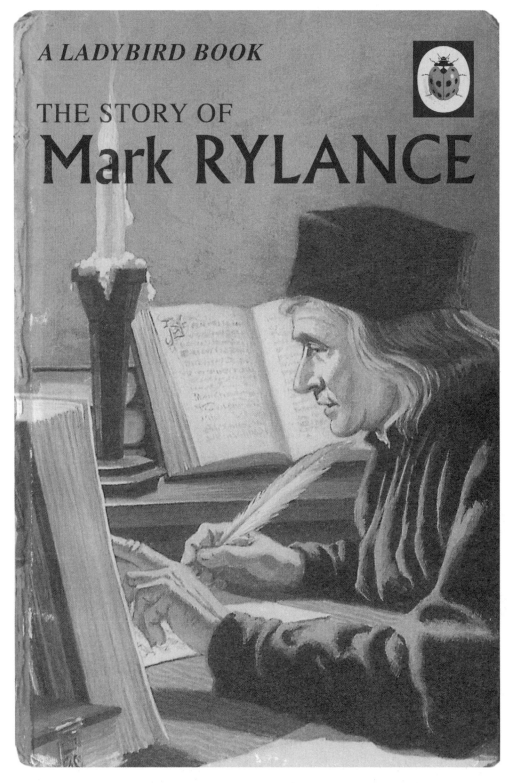

A LADYBIRD BOOK

THE STORY OF
Mark RYLANCE

Mark Rylance is meeting some of his fans at the stage door of The Globe theatre.

Mark asks them which of his plays or films they liked the best.

Then he spends half an hour preparing himself, before signing each autograph, in character.

Then he moves onto the next one.

For Mark Rylance, acting is an instinct. On stage, he cannot say what he will do from one moment to the next. He cannot explain what he does or put any of his craft into words.

Later today he will go on The Graham Norton Show and be asked to do exactly this.

It will be terrible television.

Mark Rylance is taking a break from rehearsing 'the Scottish play'.

He will not refer to this play by its name. Actors are very superstitious.

Mark has asked someone to get him a cup of tea and 'the Scottish tea-cake'.

14

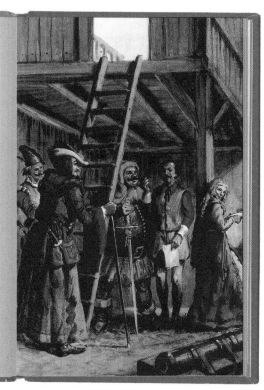

Mark Rylance is accepting his latest Academy Award for Best Supporting Actor.

He has wheeled himself onto the stage inside a pageant wagon and is performing a short scene from the Chester Mystery Cycle.

It is Mark Rylance's way of saying thank–you.

The orchestra start to play the walk–off music again, but Mark Rylance has not finished yet.

50

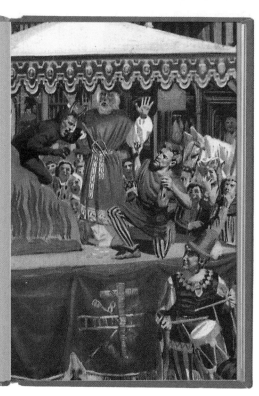

Learnabout...
Having an Affair

'How it works'

THE RACIST

A LADYBIRD BOOK

THE STORY OF
The Synth Duo
A Ladybird 'Achievements In Electronica' Book

talkabout
key performance indicators

BOTTOM RIGHT
Talkabout Key Performance Indicators contained an interactive graph of its own sales.

Grown-ups enjoy talking about people at work, and this series used a lively mixture of facts and carefully legally worded gossip to paint thumbnail portraits of these popular characters.

'People at Work'

LOUISE

A Ladybird Book

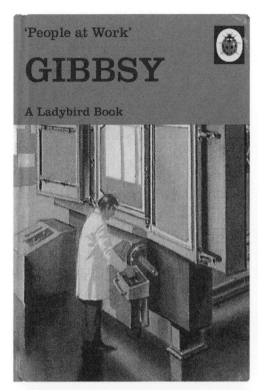

'People at Work'

GIBBSY

A Ladybird Book

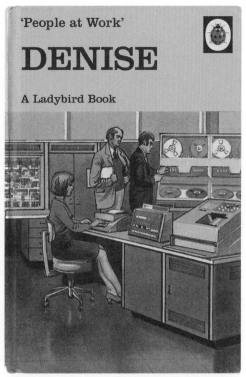

'People at Work'

DENISE

A Ladybird Book

'People at Work'

MATT

A Ladybird Book

'People at Work'

'NUTKINS'

A Ladybird Book

The *Adventures From History* series combined exciting adventure subjects with historically accurate illustrations to some effect.

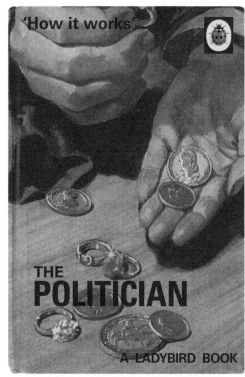

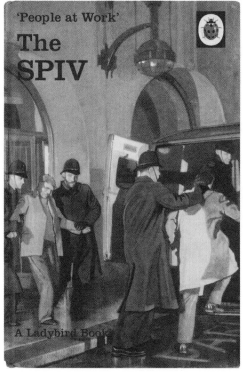

Other stories in this anthology title included *Just Good Friends* and *Brush Strokes*.

Only Fools & Horses
and other stories

British Foot Foundation

8'14P

A LADYBIRD BOOK

LADYBIRD BOOKS FOR GROWN-UPS

The recent National Sales Campaign by Beresfords Books and W.C. Ostley Heel & Key Bars for Ladybird Books For Grown-Ups has shown how much extra business can be achieved with FEATURE DISPLAYS of this fast-selling series.

MAKE UP YOUR STOCK ON THE ATTACHED B 5 ORDER FORM

WHY NOT PUT THESE BOOKS ON SHELVES IN YOUR SHOP IN CASE ANYBODY COMES IN WHO WANTS TO BUY THEM FROM YOUR SHOP?

LISTED HERE IS A LIST OF SOME BOOKS THAT YOU MAY WISH TO SELL IN YOUR SHOP FOR PEOPLE TO BUY FROM YOUR SHOP FOR MONEY

SERIES 401
RHYMING STORIES
The Good Ship Venus
The Young Man From Nantucket

SERIES 551
NATURAL HISTORY
Wasps
Life In Bins
The Beauty of Compost

SERIES 667
ACHIEVEMENTS
The Story of Darts
The Story of Toast
Bernard Bresslaw

SERIES 706
'PEOPLE AT WORK'
The Fence
The Fluffer
The Duke Of Kent

Ref No. 7657

96

THE LADYBIRD BOOK OF
THE
LUNCH BREAK

'WELL—LOVED TALES'
The
Italian Job
A LADYBIRD BOOK FOR GROWN-UPS

LADYBIRD 'ACHIEVEMENTS IN SPORT'
THE
ARMCHAIR PUNDIT

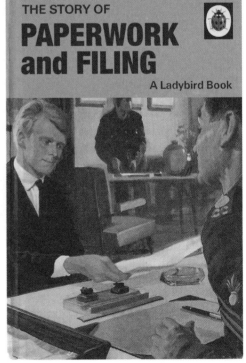

THE STORY OF
PAPERWORK
and FILING
A Ladybird Book

LADYBIRD BOOKS FOR GROWN-UPS

P.O. Box 606B, Respectable St., Framley, FM3 2LB
Tel: 0999 999999 DX: 07734

26st November

Sir Giles,

Along the lines of our telephone conversation, we would, in
principle, be very happy to issue an option in your name for
the musical rights to 'The Ladybird Book of Parents' Evening'.

Have you a composer and librettist in mind already? I seldom
go to the theatre (let alone the musical theatre), but I did
see a very engaging musical adaptation of the film 'Jaws' last
year that had some highly memorable tunes in it, especially
the one the man sung as he was being swallowed by the shark.
Maybe you could contact the team responsible? The show closed
after a week, so I imagine they're not unduly busy.

Sincerely,

K McEith

Keith McEith

New illustrations and text were often commissioned to reflect changes in sporting style in the *Ladybird For Grown-Ups* line. This book was previously *The Full-Back*.

A LADYBIRD FIRST BOOK OF

DIVING AND TIMEWASTING

talkabout
webinars

Virtue
signalling

75e

**Key Words Scheme
for Grown—Ups**

BOTTOM LEFT
The *Collecting*
series also
included *Chargers*
and *Screwdrivers*.
*Ladybird Books
For Grown-
Ups* are now
collector's items
themselves, except
these ones, which
are startlingly
unpopular.

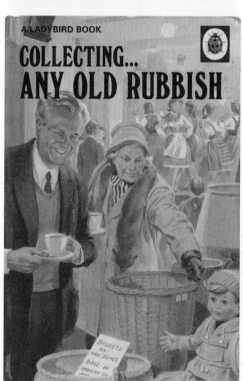

A LADYBIRD BOOK

COLLECTING...
ANY OLD RUBBISH

'Places We Go'

**THE SPEED
AWARENESS COURSE**

A LADYBIRD BOOK FOR GROWN—UPS

The *Classic Rock* series told the stories of some of rock's greatest albums from 'Once upon a time there were some Beatles…' to 'and the Velvet Underground lived happily ever after'. Fans soon noticed that the *Dark Side Of The Moon* book could be read at the same time as *The Wizard Of Oz* without improving either.

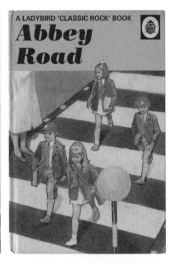

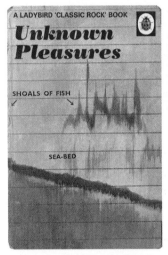

A LADYBIRD 'CLASSIC ROCK' BOOK

Dark Side Of The Moon

At Home

At Home

Home is a grown-up's favourite place. Home is where the bills are sent. Home is where the radiators need bleeding. Home is where a grown-up stays when they are recovering from an operation or medical procedure.

Most grown-ups manage to spend at least a few hours at home in the evening, when they can make the most of their dwelling by sitting in one room watching something happening to other people on a screen. Then they can go to bed before getting up again, having a shower and leaving their home.

Homes cost lots and lots of money, which is why grown-ups try not to wear them out by spending too much time there. Homes are special. Your home is at risk if you do not keep up repayments on a mortgage or other loan secured on it.

BOTTOM LEFT
The Story of Brass Eye had its publication delayed because senior management decided the book was 'not ready,' and some of the more controversial pages, like the one about the off-line edit, had to be replaced.

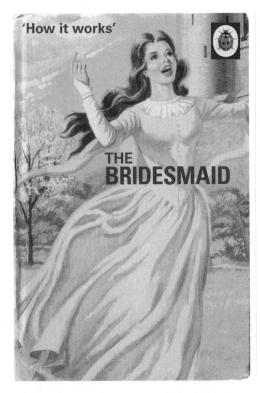

A Ladybird Book

The Argos Catalogue

Like the *Learn To Read* series, this was an attempt to fit a popular book into a format a grown-up could easily manage.

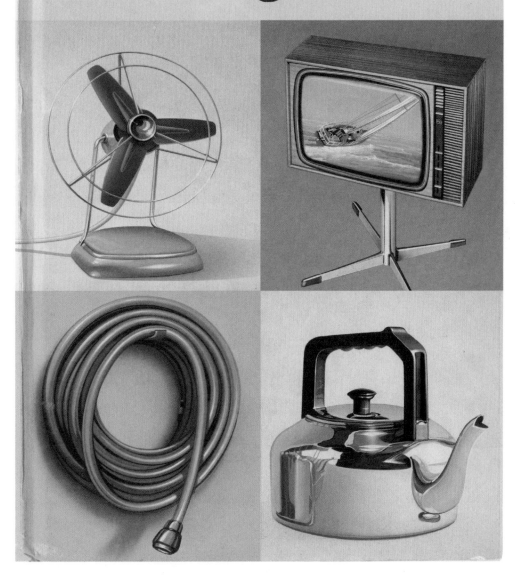

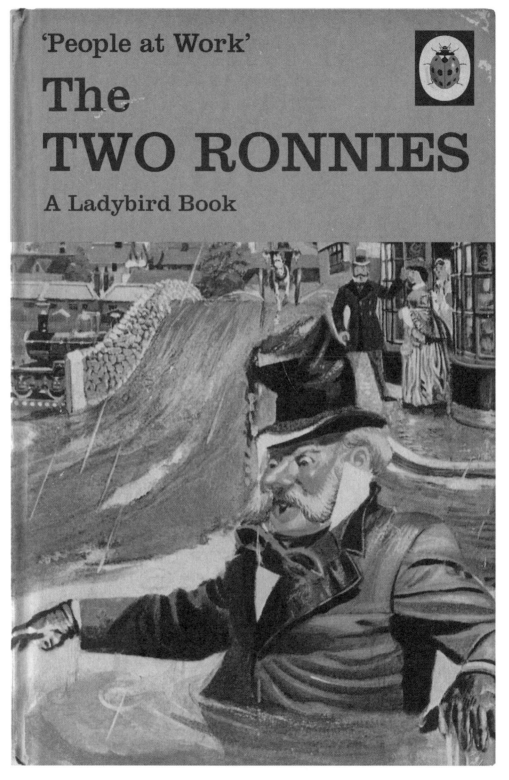

People At Work: The Two Ronnies had to be recalled after an eagle-headed reader spotted a printing error. (FACING PAGE)

'People at Work'

The TWO RONNIES

A Ladybird Book

five candles

D.P. Endsmith, author of *The Ladybird Book of The Bank Holiday*, went on to become a hospital radio magnate.

THE LADYBIRD
BOOK OF

THE
BANK HOLIDAY

"I spy with my little eye, something beginning with 'c'," says Mum.

"Cars," says Albert.

"Your turn," says Mum.

"Nearly there, kids," says Dad.

"It took longer than we planned," says Dad, "but we got here in the end."

"Hooray!" say Albert and Lucy.

"Right. Half an hour on the pier, then we have to head home," says Mum.

50

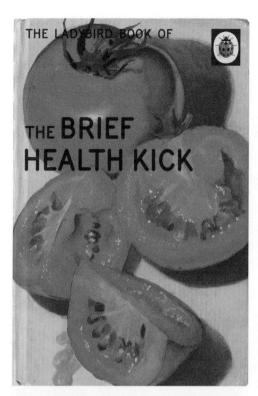

THE LADYBIRD BOOK OF

THE BRIEF
HEALTH KICK

talkabout

spoilers

BOTTOM LEFT
*Ladybird Books
For Grown-Ups*
were always
keen to address
hot-button social
issues, like risotto.

Learnabout...

Risotto

THE LADYBIRD BOOK OF

GASLIGHTING

A LADYBIRD BOOK

understanding
Curry

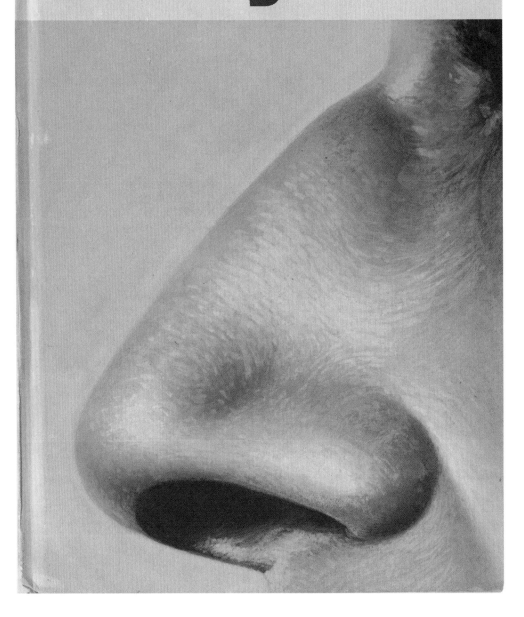

Ladybird 'Adventures In Insurance'

GREAT CLAIMS:

Kidnapped by Swans

The Ladybird Book of The Single Mum reflected the changing shape of the family, along with titles like *The Ladybird Book of Daddy's New Special Friend* and *They Know I'm Not Their Uncle.*

'How it works'

THE
SINGLE
MUM

A LADYBIRD BOOK

Laura has heard that a mother can identify her child's unique cry and would be able to lift up a car if her child had fallen under it.

On a good day, Laura would agree, but today she is so tired she has forgotten what her one looks like.

Today, Nita's son, Morve, played in his school concert. Afterwards, they went for all–you–can–eat tagliatelle and milk–shakes.

They laughed a lot, and Morve went to sleep later in Nita's bed.

Morve's father has no idea that this happened, because he is in Belize with a 21–year–old nail bar technician.

"Idiot," thinks Nita.

Mercedes's daughter has been with her father for the stipulated two days of the week.

In those two days, she appears to have become two inches taller, acquired a bicycle, and learned how to swear.

Children grow up so fast.

26

Fenella is proud of herself.

When she became a single mum, she did not know how she would do it.

But her little boy is one year old, and she did it by herself. What a year it has been.

She only has to get through seventeen more of these, and she will not be considered a failure.

50

Learning
with
Mother–in–Law

A Ladybird 'Not Like That' Book

Book 2

THE LADYBIRD BOOK OF

THE LOFT

THE LADYBIRD
BOOK OF

RAGE EATING

76c
They know we drink

The Ladybird Key Words
Scheme For Grown–Ups

TOP RIGHT
The Ladybird Book of The Loft was full of entertaining stories about ancient Christmas decorations, worthless family heirlooms, and hitting your head on the beams.

THE LADYBIRD BOOK OF

THE
ESTATE AGENT

CONSERVATION

The Carnival of Bags

Not understanding your recycling

'People at Work'

The GHOST

A Ladybird Book

A ghost does not have a mind. It does not know what it is doing. A ghost repeats simple actions again and again, for no real reason, and to no great effect.

This is why so many caretakers and fairground security guards are mistaken for ghosts.

Gryffyn and Treeve are the ghosts of two Cornish tin miners who died in an accident in 1753. They have haunted the mine ever since.

But the mine closed in 1921, and they have long since run out of people to scare. These days they mainly frighten each other.

"Whoooooooh!" says Gryffyn, spookily.

Treeve hopes a passing exorcist will fall down the mine.

How It Works: The Single Dad is thought to be the most thrown-away gift of all time.

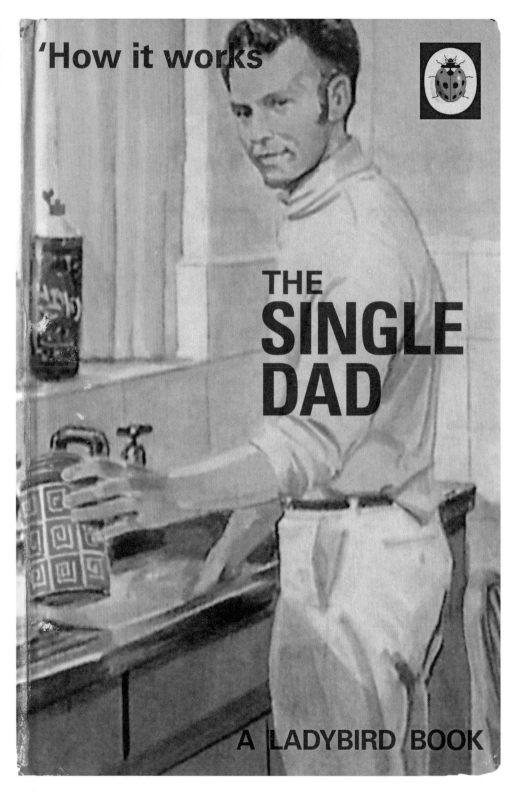

'How it works

THE
SINGLE
DAD

A LADYBIRD BOOK

Marcus's new girlfriend Lucy is not afraid of talking about the father of her children. And Marcus is very relaxed about this.

Lucy has told Marcus where her ex went to school, how he always does that thing with his toes, and what are his top six flavours of Pringle.

However, she has not told him the names or ages of her children.

"You can't rush these things," says Lucy.

8

Amir and Saskia did not want to "waste their energy" working out the child-care arrangements between them, so they decided to do it via the courts.

Six years and £20,000 later, they are reviewing the arrangements for the fifteenth time.

And still they have wasted no energy.

22

The weather is warming up, so Danny tells his children they can camp overnight in the garden.

When he looks out of the window the following morning, Danny does some very quick thinking before their mum arrives.

Within two minutes, he has come up with eleven reasons why this is not his fault, including a vendetta by someone at the Met Office.

36

It used to frustrate Declan that whenever he and Jo went out, all they talked about was their children.

Now Declan is a single dad, he no longer goes out. He stays in.

But to stop feeling lonely, he has joined twelve forums for single parents. All they talk about is their children.

44

PURCHASE ORDER

N. F. TWEBBIN

BOOKSELLER AND PRINTSUNDRYMAN
MALTHUSITER LANE, WRINGLEY

DATE   23nd May

ORDER NO.   I7085

QUANTITY	DESCRIPTION	PRICE
I2	The Ladybird Book of Folderol	
24	'People At WOrk' -- Rod Stewart	
IO	'Things To Do' -- Shouting & Screaming	
I2	'Key Words' -- He's Not Worth It	
6	'People At Work' -- The Cad	
IO	The Ladybird Book of Wife-Swapping	
4	'Great Civilisations' -- The Wombles	
6	'How It Works' -- The Freeloader	
2	'Read It Yourself' -- Finnegans Wake	
I2	The Story Of ABBA	
8	'Well-Loved Tales' -- The Profumo Affair	
8	'Key Words' -- I Knew It	
I6	The Ladybird Book of Our Robot Overlords	

RECEIVED 26 MAY 68

PURCHASING AGENT

Ladybird Books For Grown-Ups capitalised on the popularity of computer games by releasing these titles, as well as *Pong*, *Snake* and *Guitar Hero*.

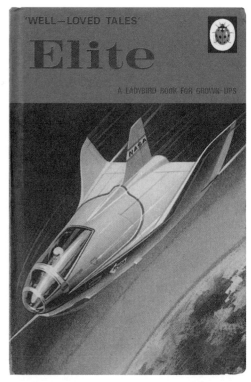

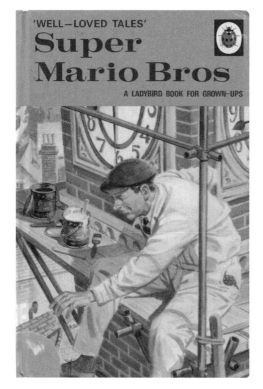

'WELL—LOVED TALES'

Grand Theft Auto 3

A LADYBIRD BOOK FOR GROWN—UPS

Coping

Coping

Coping is what a grown-up does when they find themselves under pressure from some event or person. Grown-ups are good at coping.

Grown-ups can cope with small things like having to switch to energy-saving bulbs or running out of Sellotape – and big things like losing a loved one or being attacked by a goose.

Grown-ups have things called coping mechanisms. These are ways of behaving that make them feel better when they feel under attack: things like crying, drinking, hiding, not sleeping, paying for therapy, ignoring their increasingly intolerant parents, pulling beer mats to pieces, switching off Facebook Messenger, eating too many potatoey things, and getting cross with sport.

One of the best-selling *Ladybird Books For Grown-Ups* titles ever published. Most teachers in Britain would receive at least 16 identical copies a year from their class as end-of-term gifts, and eventually some charity shops – Help The Pelvis and Welsh League For Legs (Cymru Lleag Lleg) – refused to take any more copies for fear of bursting.

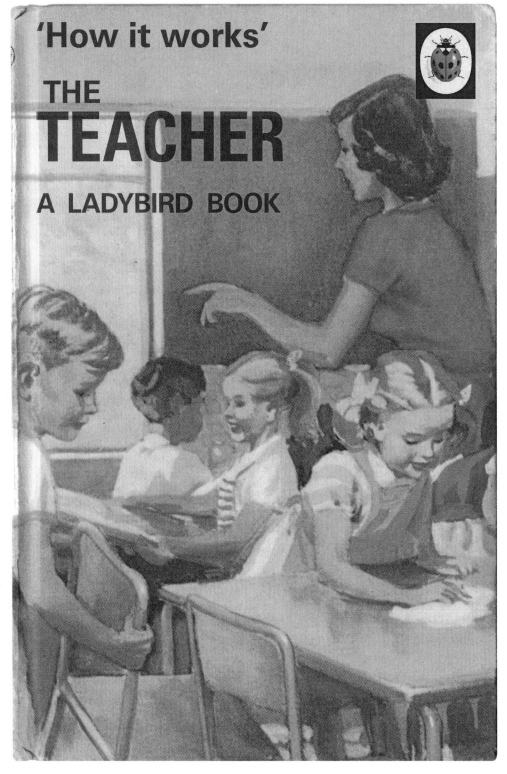

'How it works'

THE
TEACHER

A LADYBIRD BOOK

Lucy is a teacher.

She became a teacher because of a passion to shape young people's thinking and to inspire them to do the best they can.

She is currently teaching 4J the song "So Sick" by Ne–Yo.

When she started as a teacher, Carole used to read the children "The Three Little Pigs" and "We're Going On A Bear Hunt".

Now she is reading them "the success criteria for expanded column addition".

It is not as good a story.

Greg is getting to know the children in his new class. Most of them can already do up their buttons. A few of them can tie their laces.

One boy has never seen cutlery before. After the first day, his parents complain that no-one has taught him to use a knife and fork yet and threaten to sue Greg for negligence.

26

Alfie's grandmother has arrived to collect him. But Alfie's teacher has never met his grandmother, and cannot let him go with a person unknown to her.

"Granny!" says Alfie happily.

Alfie's teacher just needs to take a DNA swab from the lady to prove they are related. The results should only take four or five days.

38

"Why aren't you down the pub?" asks Mishal's friend. "You finished work at three–thirty."

Mishal left work at six o'clock. She has three hours of marking to do this evening and has to be back in work tomorrow morning at seven o'clock.

Still, at least she gets a six–week break in the summer to do a year's worth of lesson plans and have a three–day holiday in Newhaven.

Olivia's big moment of revelation comes one Thursday lunchtime as she looks out of the staff–room window.

"I have started to dream in Comic Sans," she says, out loud.

"You're one of us now," says the head of Key Stage 2.

They look at each other.

They know.

THE LADYBIRD BOOK OF
HEALTH & SAFETY LEGISLATION

Holidays in the future
69a

Key Words Scheme for Grown—Ups

A Ladybird 'Achievements' Book
Contraception

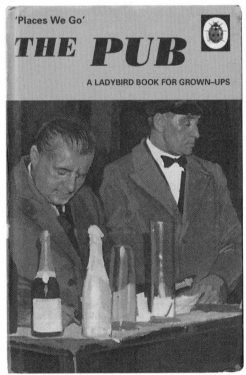

'Places We Go'
THE PUB
A LADYBIRD BOOK FOR GROWN—UPS

A LADYBIRD BOOK

'TALES FROM THE BOX–SETS'

BREAKING BAD

Another popular title by D. E. F. Gee, the author of *How It Works: The Teacher* and *How To Make Your Own Petrol*.

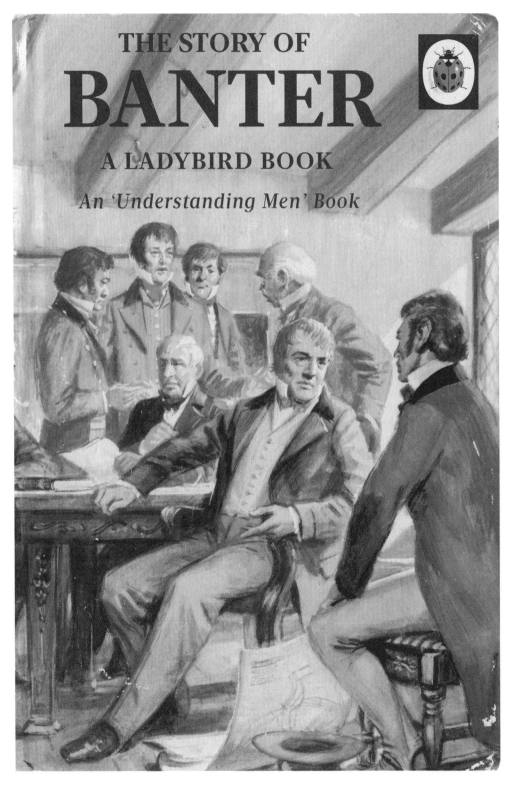

An edition of this book, translated into banter, was a best-seller in Basildon.

THE STORY OF
BANTER

A LADYBIRD BOOK

An 'Understanding Men' Book

THE LADYBIRD BOOK OF

PILATES

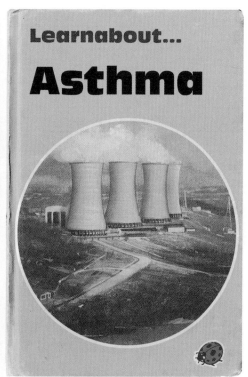

Learnabout...

Asthma

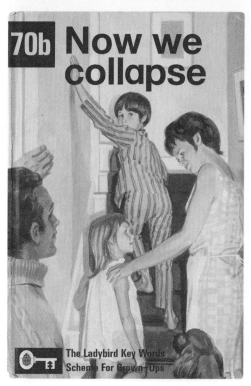

70b Now we collapse

The Ladybird Key Words
Scheme For Grown-Ups

A LADYBIRD BOOK

'TALES FROM THE BOX–SETS'
THE SOPRANOS

TOP LEFT
The Ladybird Book of Pilates replaced the earlier title *The Ladybird Book of Physical Jerks*.

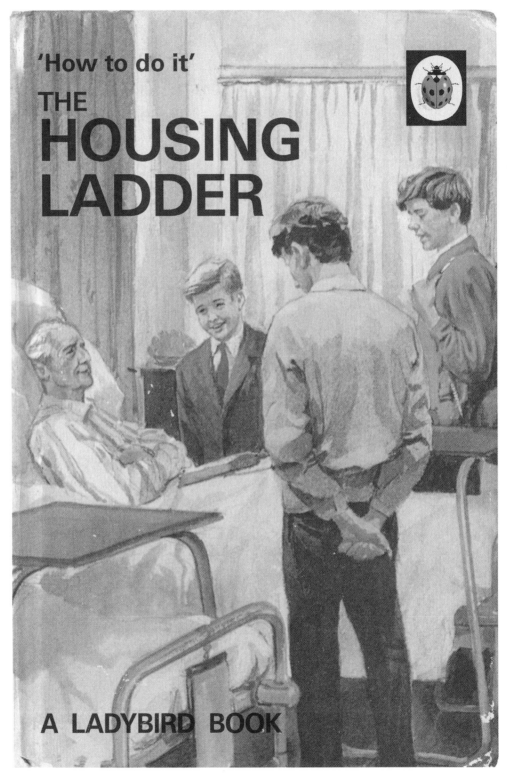

'How to do it'

THE
HOUSING
LADDER

A LADYBIRD BOOK

Imagine a balloon full of people, rising up, up, up. The people in the balloon wave happily. They paid a lot of money for the ride.

There is no way up to the balloon. There used to be a ladder. There is not a ladder now. There is only a balloon.

"Surely the balloon will burst soon" think the people on the ground. "Then we can get on."

The balloon rises into the sky. For ever.

6

Balliol and Waris started renting their flat in 2003, when putting down a deposit to buy it would have been perfectly affordable on their salaries.

Now the flat is worth millions. Balliol wishes he had a time machine.

But all his time machine researching money has been wasted on renting their flat.

12

Learnabout Paganism proved to be a popular Imbolc, Samhain or Beltane gift.

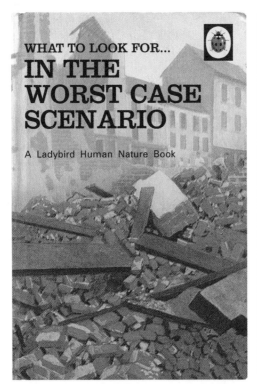

WHAT TO LOOK FOR...
IN THE WORST CASE SCENARIO

A Ladybird Human Nature Book

Learnabout...

Paganism

THE LADYBIRD BOOK OF

BROMANCE

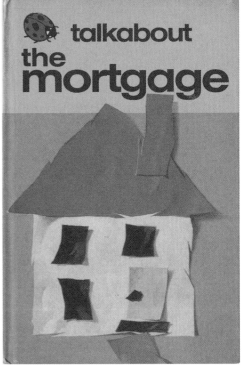

talkabout
the mortgage

86a Dad's gone

The Ladybird Key Words
Scheme For Grown–Ups

The *Key Words Scheme for Grown-Ups* introduced readers to many basic legal terms.

This title, written by Mrs L. M. Longcraig, had the longest, most detailed commissioning document in Ladybird history.

THE LADYBIRD BOOK OF

MANSPLAINING

Sometimes Mansford does not feel he is being treated as importantly as he should.

To make these feelings go away, Mansford likes to explain something to a nearby woman, preferably something that she already understands very well.

"This," Mansford explains, "is called mansplaining."

"If you ask me, what you should have done there is played a direct game into the wide channels — plus Pendle should have started upfront and you need more structure in your midfield," says Ricky to the captain of the England women's national football team.

She did not ask him.

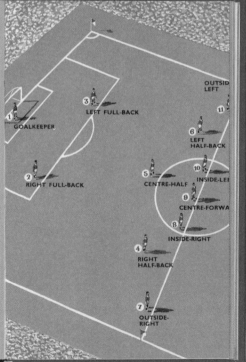

Covers were often redrawn to reflect changing times, changing attitudes, and the changing size of domestic ovens.

A LADYBIRD 'EASY READING' BOOK

'People at Work'

THE SOCIAL SERVICES

'People at Work'

SOCIAL
SERVICES

A Ladybird Book

Author Dr J. D. Ptetherick was the perfect choice for this book, being medically afraid of flying, boats, flying boats, passports, paella and non-imperial measurements.

THE LADYBIRD BOOK OF
THE BRITISH HOLIDAY

Before we go on holiday, the car needs to be packed.

Mum packs the suitcases and the beach towels and the rain–coats and the swimming costumes and the scarves and jumpers and the flip–flops and the sun–block and the Deep Heat and the buckets and spades and the board games. It all fits in very nicely.

Then Dad unpacks it all and does it again, a different way. "It won't fit otherwise," he says.

8

"There really is nothing better than a lovely sunny beach," says Dad, looking at the finished jigsaw of a lovely sunny beach.

Outside, it sounds like the hailstones have got heavier.

38

It is raining again, but there are plenty of things to see at the National Pin Cushion Collection in Llandrindod Wells.

And if it rains again tomorrow, there will still be plenty of things to see at the National Pin Cushion Collection in Llandrindod Wells.

44

When we get home, it is good to remember the time we all had.

"It is surprising how rain does not show up on photographs," says Dad.

50

GEORGIAN
THELMA &
LOUISE

A LADYBIRD 'Adventure from History'

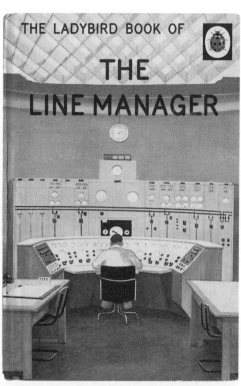

THE LADYBIRD BOOK OF

THE
LINE MANAGER

The Ladybird Book of
Diabetes

Learnabout...

Arson

The Ladybird Book of The Line Manager was sent into space aboard the ESA probe Grimaldi to lower alien expectations of Earth culture.

Learnabout...

Pot Noodle

Ladybird Books for Grown—Ups

P.O. Box 606B   Respectable St.   Framley–On–The–Land
Hereshire   FM3 2LB   *Reg. office*

Telephone: 099-99 99999 (6 lines)   *Telegrams:* Grown-Ups Framley England
Reg. no. 55318008 England

31st Juny

Dear Mr Alliot,

Thank you for your unsolicited submission 'The Story of
Michael Bloody Wendover'. We do, as you say in your covering
letter, publish a series of books on the subject of figures of
interest, but I must admit I had never heard of Mr Wendover.

On reading your manuscript, I wondered whether the short
format of our books had perhaps caused you to omit whichever
achievement you consider has merited Mr Wendover a place in
our series alongside other best-selling titles on the likes of
Winston Churchill, Lulu and Giant Haystacks.

Am I correct in guessing that Mr Wendover is your next-door
neighbour? It would certainly explain the aggressive tone of
your text.

Sadly, I shall have to pass.

Sir Nelson Wriddle

These two titles were also published in splash-proof editions.

THE LADYBIRD BOOK OF

THE STAG DO

THE LADYBIRD BOOK OF

THE HEN PARTY

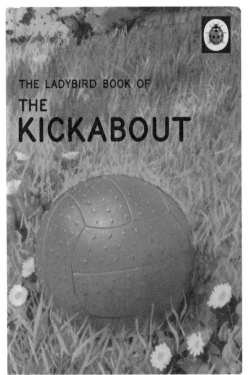

THE LADYBIRD BOOK OF
THE
KICKABOUT

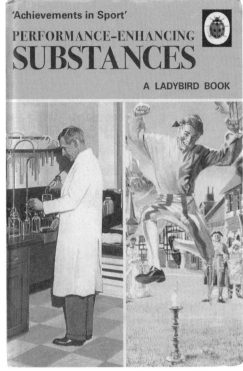

'Achievements in Sport'
PERFORMANCE-ENHANCING
SUBSTANCES
A LADYBIRD BOOK

83c **Holidays are long**

The Ladybird Key Words
Scheme For Grown-Ups

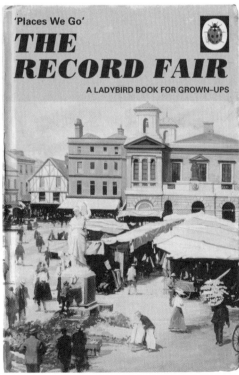

'Places We Go'
**THE
RECORD FAIR**
A LADYBIRD BOOK FOR GROWN-UPS

'How it works'

THE
BORN–AGAIN
CHRISTIAN

A LADYBIRD BOOK

Plans to distribute this book door-to-door were shelved after complaints from absolutely everyone.

Not Coping

Not Coping

Grown-ups are awfully busy. But sometimes they stop being busy and stare out of the window with an expression on their face like someone watching a snowman melt on purpose. This is called Not Coping.

You can tell when a grown-up is not coping because they stop doing the things they should be doing, and do other things they would not usually do, like tidy the shed or get extra hair or buy expensive tickets to a gig by a band from the 1990s that they had no interest in seeing at the time or have their portrait painted in oils or learn the harpsichord or move to the Fens.

Not coping is even more fun than coping, because it is usually done faster, in a higher pitched voice with occasional crying jags. Not coping is lots of things, but it is certainly not boring.

It is also a sign that there are only two things to do: change something or give up. And, of course, most grown-ups can only change things with a lot of effort. So they give up.

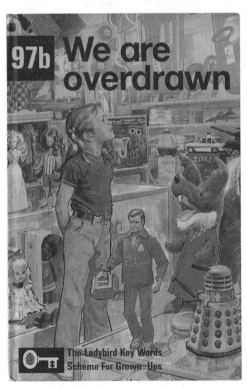

'WELL—LOVED TALES'

Get Carter

A LADYBIRD BOOK FOR GROWN—UPS

Learnabout...

Embarrassment

'Places We Go'

THE CONFERENCE

A LADYBIRD BOOK FOR GROWN–UPS

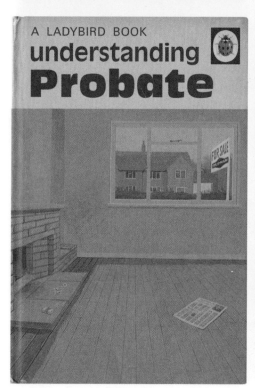

A LADYBIRD BOOK

understanding **Probate**

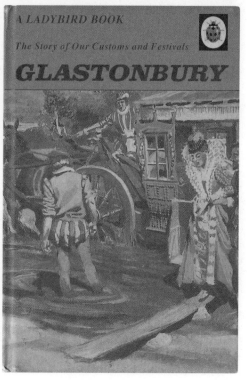

A LADYBIRD BOOK

The Story of Our Customs and Festivals

GLASTONBURY

BOTTOM RIGHT
The *Customs And Festivals* series also included *Pride, The Notting Hill Carnival* and *The Mawferry Box Smashing And Wake.*

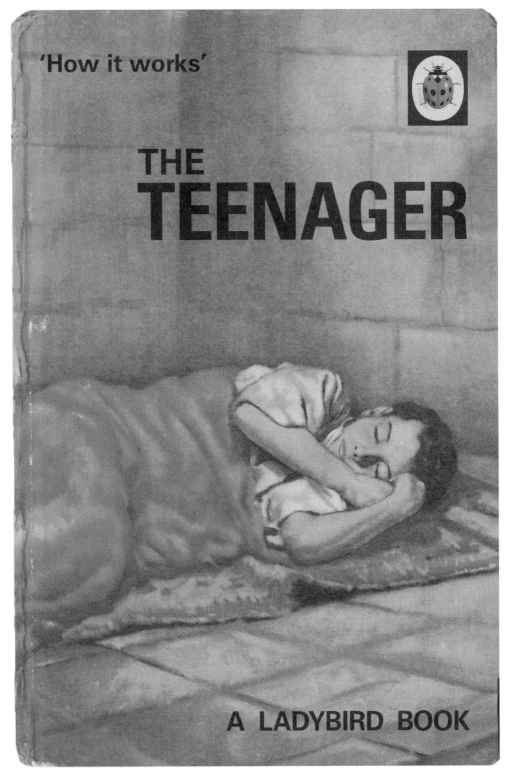

How It Works: The Teenager had its initial print run pulped due to concerns about how unhygienic it smelled.

'How it works'

THE
TEENAGER

A LADYBIRD BOOK

Max is thirteen.

Every day, Max goes to the fridge many times. He takes things out of the fridge and puts them in his mouth without thinking.

"Where has all the milk gone?" asks Max. "Mum! We've run out of ham," he shouts.

Max has no idea where the things come from. He does not know where they go. He only knows that they keep running out.

10

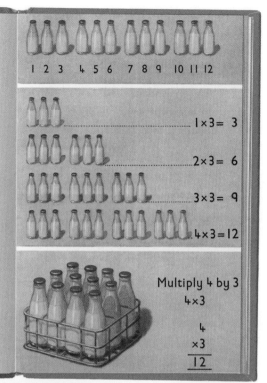

Bunthorne's mother knows he will need his smart shoes tomorrow.

Bunthorne knows where one of his shoes is. He says the other is under "my stuff".

His mother must not touch his stuff. But Bunthorne cannot really be bothered to look himself.

He thinks any Saturday job that turns someone down for hopping into the interview room is probably committing a hate crime.

22

"You can't go out dressed like that," says Gabriela's mother.

She is very upset. Partly by the clothes, but mainly by how much she sounds like her own mother.

12

Janina's mother has a weekly cocktail–night with her friends. She always boasts that she never has a hangover afterwards.

This is because her cocktail–night usually ends at 8.45pm after two lime–and–sodas, when she has to drive to pick up her scowling, grunting daughter from wherever it is this time.

16

Ladybird Books for Grown—Ups

P.O. Box 606B   Respectable St.   Framley–On–The–Land
Hereshire   FM3 2LB *Reg. office*

Telephone: 099-99 99999 (6 lines)   *Telegrams:* Grown-Ups Framley England
Reg. no. 55318008 England

20nd March

My dear Ralph,

    Delighted as I am to receive your six new Ladybird Books
for Grown-Ups (having only asked for one!), I cannot in all
responsibility let them go without comment.

    For example, your book on Ted Heath seems to me to contain
a number of assertions that may lack veracity. Firstly, that
our former P.M. could fly. Secondly, that he had the capacity
to spin cobwebs from his wrists and scale tall buildings using
only his bare hands and feet. And, perhaps most pressingly,
that he 'went big and green when he got cross'.

    Might it be that you have been watching several exciting
television programmes while writing the book and somehow
confused them with the matter at hand?

    By the by, you included the blueprints to your home-
made hovercraft with the last typescript. I will ensure my
secretary returns these to you post haste.

Sir Nelson Wriddle

The British
Association Of
Narcissists were
consulted for
this book, but it
proved difficult to
get them to engage
with the subject
matter because
they insisted
on giving the
author repeated
guided tours of
their offices and
showing him
photographs of the
time they met The
Duke of Bristol.

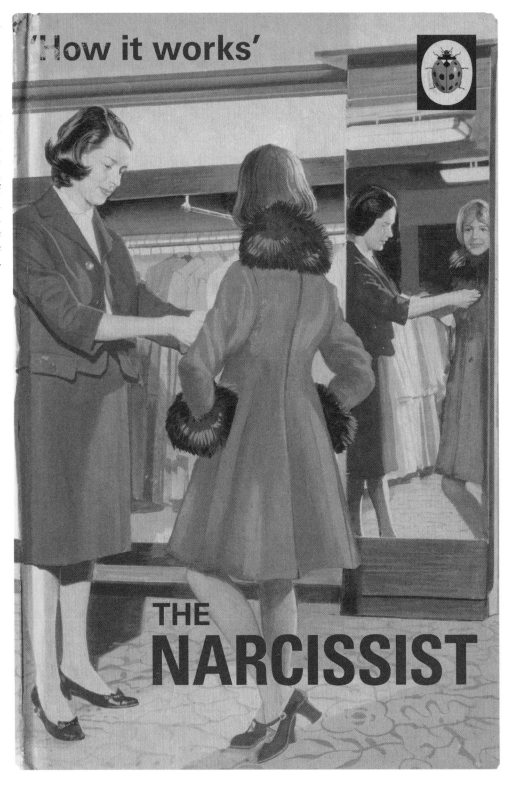

'How it works'

THE
NARCISSIST

"This is my best friend Sally," says Heather.

Heather met Sally two weeks ago. Sally seemed impressed with something Heather did or said to appear impressive.

In a few months' time, Heather will have yet another new best friend.

At the funeral, Alan spent over half an hour telling his brother's widow all about how much work he had done on his house by himself and how good the new kitchen was looking and how the neighbours were terribly jealous of it.

"I'm sure it cheered her up," he thinks to himself afterwards, although he did not think this at the time and, even now, does not realise he doesn't believe it.

A LADYBIRD BOOK

making a Basic iPhone

'Through The Ages'

MIXING YOUR DRINKS

A Ladybird Book

BOTTOM LEFT *Places We Go: Ibiza* was a bestseller for several summers, before it was overtaken by *Places We Go: Faliraki.*

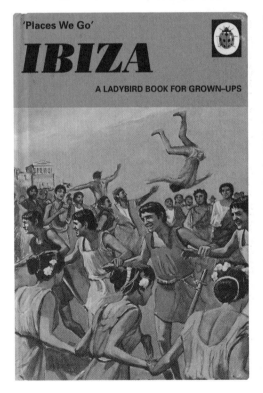

'Places We Go'

IBIZA

A LADYBIRD BOOK FOR GROWN-UPS

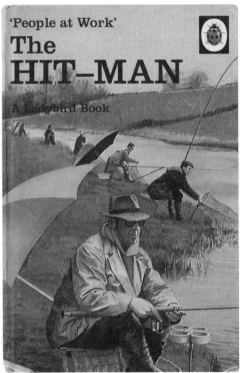

'People at Work'

The HIT-MAN

A Ladybird Book

'WELL—LOVED TALES'

Threads

A LADYBIRD BOOK FOR GROWN—UPS

Well-Loved Tales: Threads was discussed in cabinet, as papers released under the thirty-year rule later showed. There were demands to remove the picture of the lady in the shopping centre, but the publishers resisted.

Your life is short. If your existence has any meaning, which it may not, it will be to do with your relationship with those you love.

But everyone you love will one day die. Just as you will die.

So what is the point?

The night—time is a good time to doubt everything.

6

Yesterday, Stanleigh banged his ankle against the coffee table. He did not worry about it in the day, because it was day.

At 1am, he brushes the bruise against the bed—frame and wakes up in the dark.

He tries getting himself back to sleep by Googling "is there such a thing as ankle cancer?", but it is not helping.

40

"What's going on here, then?" asks the policeman.

"The conceptual frame-work of my life has collapsed," says Ted. "All existence is aimless, and what my senses define as reality is without purpose, shape or function."

The policeman asks the question again. Ted can see he is crying.

22

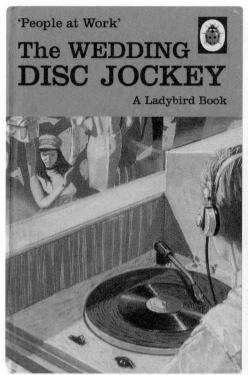

'People at Work'

The WEDDING DISC JOCKEY

A Ladybird Book

'WELL—LOVED TALES'

Lorem Ipsum Dolor

A LADYBIRD BOOK FOR GROWN-UPS

THE LADYBIRD BOOK OF

THE ATKINS DIET

'People at Work'

The VLOGGER

A Ladybird Book

TOP RIGHT
Well-Loved Tales: Lorem Ipsum Dolor is the rarest *Ladybird Book For Grown-Ups*, the entire thing being the result of a catastrophic printing error. Copies these days change hands for as much as £4,800,000.

The Key Words edition of *Passive Aggression* divided opinion. Several bookshops refused to stock it, and told customers they could go and find another bookshop if they wanted a copy that badly.

Passive aggression

ook

Key Words Scheme for Grown–Ups

"The harbour has moved," Noel shouts to the ship's captain. "It is now two miles up the coast."

"Then they'll just have to move it back," shouts the captain. "This is my spot and I always moor here."

"I didn't want that job with the stupid Forestry Commission anyway," thinks Norbert, as he hacks into another protected tree.

how to make
Your Own
Cigars

Crisps for dinner

92c

 Key Words Scheme for Grown-Ups

Derek Jarman's film *Blue* was adapted into many forms, including this book, a musical and a rollercoaster ride at Funwood Pleasures theme park.

'WELL—LOVED TALES'

Derek Jarman's 'Blue'

A LADYBIRD BOOK FOR GROWN—UPS

Derek has been to the hospital.

His doctor tells him that his eyes are permanently damaged.

He may never see again.

But his film is very good.

6

Derek reflects on how one day we will all be forgotten — our names, our work, our lives.

He even thinks that the colour blue will eventually die.

What do you think?

52

Giving Up

Giving Up

In the end, every grown-up gives up.

Everything is, eventually, too much. Eating to feel happy makes you feel unhappy. Trying to do better at everything makes you too tired to try anything. Flowers die. Pets die. Children love you, then detest you, then abandon you, then ask you for money, then abandon you again.

Every career ends in unemployment. Every hair goes grey or falls out. Every meal goes cold. Every bright colour fades. Every fabric rots or gets eaten by moths. Every footstep slowly destroys a shoe. Every sleep gradually ruins a mattress. Everything you hold important will one day not matter at all.

Your enthusiasm gives up. Your libido gives up. Your friends give up.

And you give up as well. Because giving up is what grown-ups do.

Sometimes there is no point trying any longer. But you can enjoy giving up.

This book was also published in a chart-bottoming e-book edition.

Adventures in Computing

FORGETTING YOUR PASSWORD

A LADYBIRD BOOK

Every time your computer does something new, it asks you to think of a password.

The computer says your new password must be hard to guess.

But instead of choosing a password that is hard to guess, you have picked a password that is hard to remember.

Again.

Recently, Oscar's cloud storage provider changed its rules for passwords. Oscar can no longer use "elizabeth7". He must use big and small letters, as well as numbers and symbols.

He suspects his password is almost certainly "3L1>ab3th7" or definitely "EL!7a83TH7eVeN". Or possibly something else.

Oscar wrote the password on a document, and stored it safely in his cloud storage, but sadly he cannot remember his password.

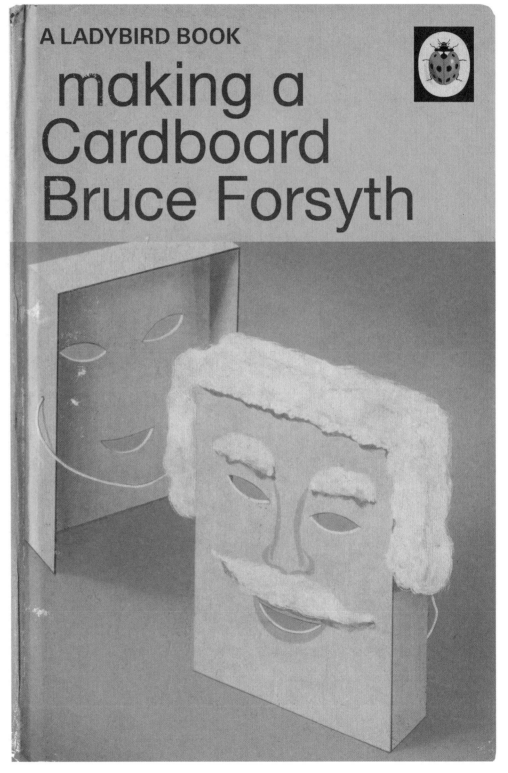

Readers who made the model detailed in this book were surprised to discover that the finished build stood a heart-stopping 11 feet (3.35m) tall.

A LADYBIRD BOOK

making a Cardboard Bruce Forsyth

The mechanism

Your cardboard Bruce Forsyth will need lots of cogs to make him move.

Use the boxes from cream–cheese triangles. Wrap corrugated cardboard round the edges.

When one cog moves, the cog connected to it will move (see page 24) and your cardboard Bruce Forsyth will get into his trademark 'Thinker' pose – or do the soft–shoe shuffle.

The moustache

Your cardboard Bruce Forsyth will need a moustache.

You can use cotton–wool, like you did for the hair.

Or if you cannot afford that much cotton–wool, simply cut the edge of some paper into a feathered patten, using a pair of safety scissors.

Whichever method you use, your cardboard Bruce Forsyth will look every inch the consummate cardboard Mr Saturday Night.

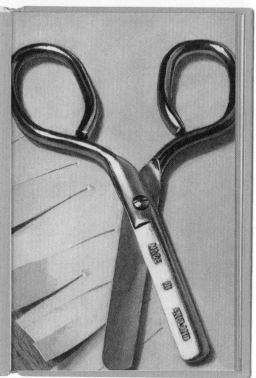

TOP LEFT
The simplified text in this *Read It Yourself* book was approved by the original author and written by Dexy's Midnight Runners.

read it your self

Time's Arrow

05 level gnidaer

'People at Work'

CHRIS EVANS

A Ladybird Book

The Ladybird Book of
Spending Their Inheritance

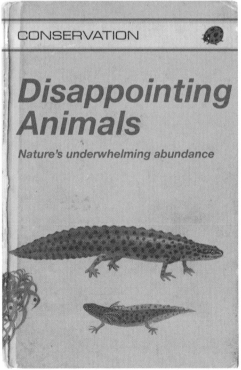

CONSERVATION

Disappointing Animals

Nature's underwhelming abundance

LADYBIRD
LEADERS

dry january

Author H. D. Shinglesmith was a reformed bellringer and alcoholic.

Stories of Britain's colourful and mysterious rituals were always popular with overseas readers.

A LADYBIRD BOOK

The Story of Our Customs and Festivals

Jools Holland's HOOTENANNY

"Coming up now, fresh from their North American tour, the fabulous Sharon Jones and the Dap Kings," said the little man, dancing on the spot.

"No more," cried the princess. "No more music."

But the music would not stop.

The princess was so very tired that she feared her heart would stop.

"No more, please," she begged. But the little man said his magic words again.

"Boogie–woogie!" laughed the little man. "Boogie–woogie!"

And the music did not stop.

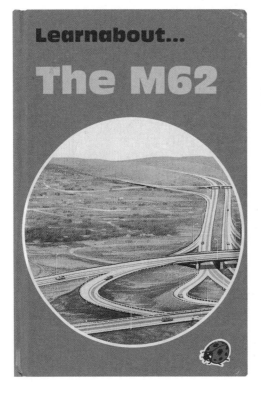

talkabout how you got here

Small-talk was just one of the core skills *Ladybird Books For Grown-Ups* sought to develop in its readers.

This revised version of *The Ladybird Book of The One-Night Stand* was entirely repainted, with the GIs, floozies and Teddy Boys of the first edition replaced by a more contemporary mix of medallion men, crumpet and Jack-the-Lads.

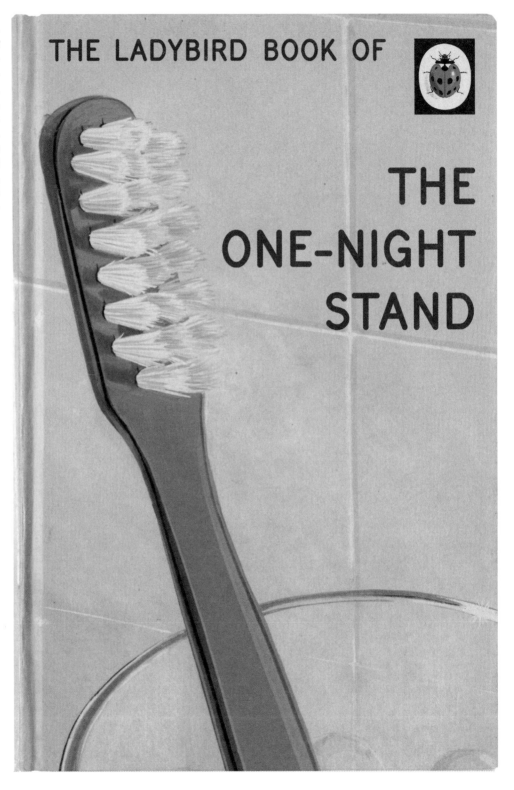

THE LADYBIRD BOOK OF

THE ONE-NIGHT STAND

Karen and Nigel met last night at a party and went home together.

This morning, they are both wondering whether to see each other again.

Karen goes to leave. "Good—bye, Neil," she says to Nigel.

"Good—bye, Katy," he replies.

They will probably not see each other again.

10

Lydia regrets what happened after she met Damon.

They went back to Damon's flat, one thing led to another, and they ended up discussing Byron until four o'clock in the morning.

Lydia has only discussed Byron once before, as part of a long and loving relationship. Now she feels dirty.

"Still," thinks Lydia, "at least Byron would have approved."

52

BOTTOM LEFT
The Hypochondriac is one of the least-borrowed Ladybird titles from public libraries, but the most frequently washed.

THE LADYBIRD BOOK OF

HUMAN INSIGNIFICANCE

THE LADYBIRD BOOK OF

THOU HAST BEEN FAITHFUL UNTO DEATH

THE
FLING

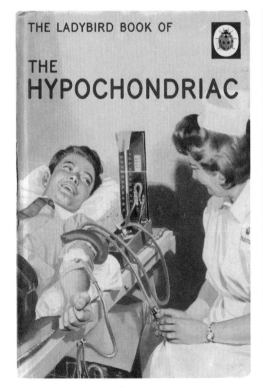

THE LADYBIRD BOOK OF

THE
HYPOCHONDRIAC

Sunday is boring

96b

Key Words Scheme for Grown-Ups

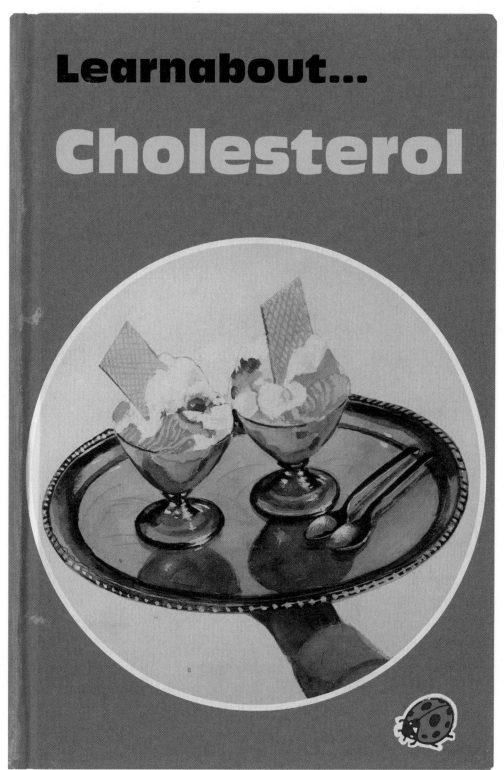

Learnabout...
Cholesterol

Much of the medical advice in this book (avoid thin food, drink hot tapwater, eat more fox) now seems charmingly old-fashioned.

The author, K. S. LaRonette wrote only one more title, *The Story Of Our Skirting Boards,* before succumbing to a fatal bout of ennui.

A LADYBIRD BOOK

understanding
Ennui

Rok is in his cabin at the depot.
He is writing down his feelings.
His ex–wife said that might help.

"Bored," he writes. "Flat. Aimless.
Weary. Listless. Desolate."

He looks at the word "listless".
"But I'm not listless," thinks Rok.
"I have this list."

Rok laughs, but a sound comes
out like crying.

10

Every time Danton goes shopping
he takes the same walk through
the underpass. The underpass is
always the same.

Today he notices the council have
painted a colourful new mural of
a jazz band on the underpass.

Danton kicks the mural.

Change is the only thing Danton
hates more than ennui.

24

A real curiosity. If you look closely, you may notice a minor typesetting error has affected this first edition of *At The Library*. Luckily the mistake was spotted after only 240,000 copies were printed, and despite this imperfection, the book remains one of the best-selling titles in the *Ladybird Books For Grown-Ups* line.

A LADYBIRD BOOK

AT THE
LIBREMONY

Tremony at the library

CROWLAND'S Silver Jubilee committee was finally wound up on Thursday evening with a presentation ceremony at the library.

The jubilee fund, described by chairman Frank Parnell as 'one of the finest efforts in Lincolnshire', fremony at the library.

The jubilee fund, described by chairman Frank Parnell as 'one remony atremony aremony at the library.

The jubremony at the library.

Tremony at remony at the library

Jubremony at the libremony

Thrremony at tremony at the libremony at the libraremony at the library.

Theremony at the library.

The jubilee fund, described by chairman Frank Premony rremony at the remony aremony at the libremony atremony at the tremony at the library.

Tremorremony at the library remony at the library.

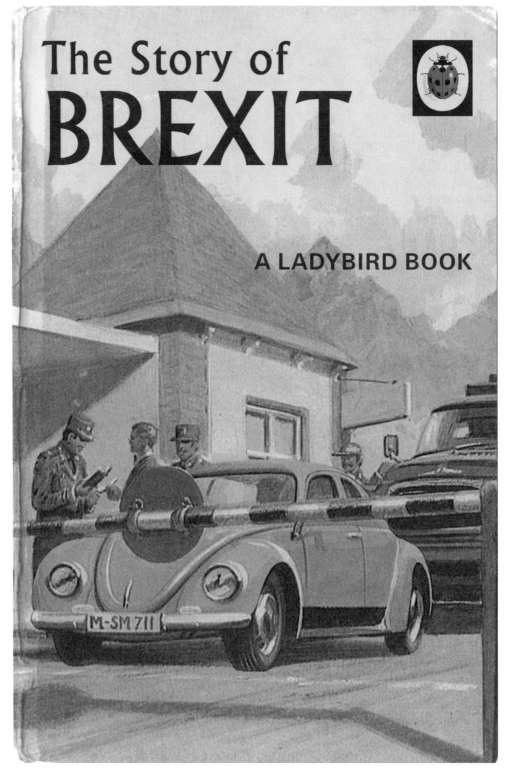

A complicated, confusing process which could be explained perfectly in the *Ladybird Books For Grown-Ups* style, *Brexit* was an unarguable success.

The Story of
BREXIT

A LADYBIRD BOOK

Europe is very different from Britain.

For instance, their windows open inwards rather than outwards and it is almost impossible to buy Monster Munch in Bulgaria.

No wonder we could not get along.

6

Like a lot of his friends, Iggy was not very interested in European federal politics. He did not know whether to vote Remain or Leave.

He was hoping there would be a third option to kick the Prime Minister out of a window.

He would have happily ticked that box.

12

Cornwallis tells everybody that he has got his country back.

He has even started a private militia to deal with "anyone trying to enter the village who does not know the fourth verse of the National Anthem".

In the first week, he had interned thirty–eight "undesirable types," including his own plumber.

44

"Leaving was the will of the people," sighs Angelica's father. He voted to leave.

Angelica voted to remain, but she feels the same way. "It is the will of the people," she sighs.

They stare at the ducks. They like the ducks. Ducks are better than people.

16

THE LADYBIRD BOOK OF

THE
TRIAL
SEPARATION

53c They are bored

The Ladybird Key Words
Scheme For Grown-Ups

Some Dreadful Men And Women was withdrawn after legal pressure from Claire. A revised edition replaced her with Idi Amin.

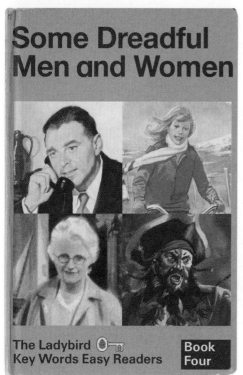

Some Dreadful
Men and Women

The Ladybird
Key Words Easy Readers

Book
Four

A LADYBIRD BOOK

What to look for
UNDERNEATH
YOUR DOG

Brand consultants had reported declining engagement with traditional fairy-tales amongst the line's target demographic, and a set of 32 new story books, based on popular viral internet memes such as *Cat Bin Lady*, *Two Girls One Cup* and *Rickrolling* were produced, selling a total of 42 copies before being withdrawn under police escort.

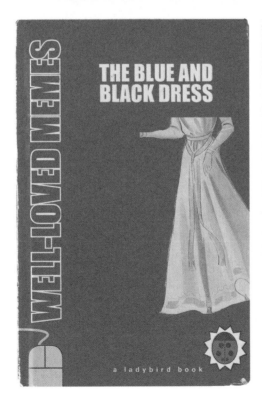

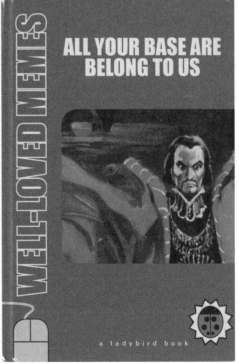

I CAN HAZ
CHEESBURGER?

WELL-LOVED MEMES

a ladybird book

'Places We Go'

HEAD OFFICE

A LADYBIRD BOOK FOR GROWN–UPS

LADYBIRD BOOKS FOR GROWN—UPS · FRAMLEY

101 Respectable Street · *Framley-On-The-Land* · *Hereshire*

TELEPHONE / RE—DIRECTION SERVICE · FRAMLEY 606

22rd July

Dear Johnnie --

    Please accept my most sincere apologies for the wait
weighted to this reply.

    If I may ask, when might we see a copy of the
manuscript of "The Ladybird Book Of Procrastination"? It
has been some time in the coming and is, I am sure you will
understand, now a considerable distance over-due.

Yours aye,

F Muttes

Nelson Wriddle
pp

Ladybird Books For Grown-Ups published several souvenir titles commemorating significant national events, including the launch of the Kia Sorento and the wedding of Scott and Charlene in *Neighbours*.

Blur vs Oasis

Chin Concern

Op

Chinny Good Value!

A Ladybird souvenir of Brit-Pop

Ladybird Books for Grown—Ups
P.O. Box 606B Respectable St. Framley–On–The–Land
Hereshire FM3 2LB *Reg. office*

Telephone: 099-99 99999 (6 lines) *Telegrams:* Grown-Ups Framley England
Reg. no. 55318008 England

1th March

Dear Johnnie,

    Thank you, most sinceriously, for the first four pages of
'The Ladybird Book Of Procrastination'. The eight-year gap
between its commission and this arrival has certainly been
worth the wait. Might you have any idea when the rest shall
arrive upon me?

Yours aye,

Sir Nelson Wriddle
PP

This book, like many featured here, is from a time when books were proper books, and the sun was always shining and toys were built to last and Wagon Wheels were bigger and nobody expected something for nothing and kids didn't answer back – a kinder world; a better world – and fetches up to 10p in charity shops.

THE LADYBIRD BOOK OF

Nostalgia
and Wistfulness

PLEASE HELP
£0.01p
SCOTTISH HAIR RELIEF

LADYBIRD BOOKS FOR GROWN-UPS

P.O. Box 606B, Respectable St., Framley, FM3 2LB
Tel: 0999 999999 DX: 07734

18st August

John,

As you know, it has been some decades now since we entered
into a contract for The Ladybird Book Of Procrastination and
we remain yet to receive the finished script.

Could you advise us as to when we can expect it? Sir Nelson
died eleven years ago, and though he would have liked to see
the book in print in his life-time, maybe we can compromise,
in that I see it in mine?

Sincerely,

K McEith

Keith McEith

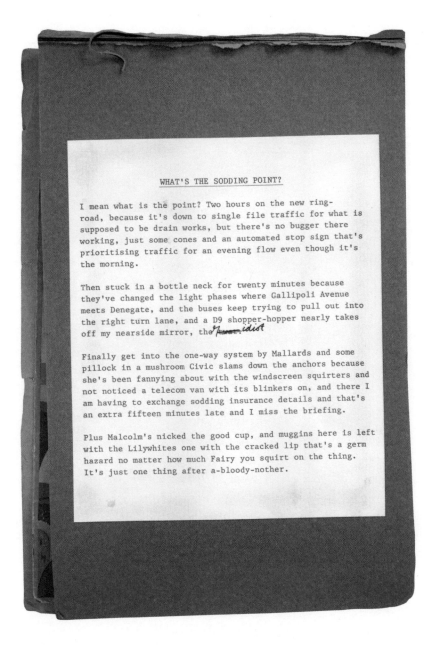

WHAT'S THE SODDING POINT?

I mean what is the point? Two hours on the new ring-road, because it's down to single file traffic for what is supposed to be drain works, but there's no bugger there working, just some cones and an automated stop sign that's prioritising traffic for an evening flow even though it's the morning.

Then stuck in a bottle neck for twenty minutes because they've changed the light phases where Gallipoli Avenue meets Denegate, and the buses keep trying to pull out into the right turn lane, and a D9 shopper-hopper nearly takes off my nearside mirror, the ~~fucking~~ idiot

Finally get into the one-way system by Mallards and some pillock in a mushroom Civic slams down the anchors because she's been fannying about with the windscreen squirters and not noticed a telecom van with its blinkers on, and there I am having to exchange sodding insurance details and that's an extra fifteen minutes late and I miss the briefing.

Plus Malcolm's nicked the good cup, and muggins here is left with the Lilywhites one with the cracked lip that's a germ hazard no matter how much Fairy you squirt on the thing. It's just one thing after a-bloody-nother.

Explaining the world to grown-ups could take its toll on even the strongest minds. This unpublished title, by one of the imprint's most prolific authors, was over 200 pages long. The author, who cannot be named for the usual reasons, submitted this layout, before shaving off all his clothes and becoming the bass player in The Gingerbread Authority (a name readers may recognise from the sleevenotes to the original cast recording of controversial Dutch musical *Bums*). He was never heard of again.

The Artists

John Berry
Harry Wingfield
Martin Aitchison
Robert Ayton
Bernard H. Robinson
Gerald Witcomb
Eric Winter
Frank Hampson
Frank Humphris
John Kenney
Jack Matthew
Roger Hall
Kenneth Inns
Ron Embleton
Ronald Lampitt
Jorge Núñez
Harry Woolley
David Carey
Robert Lumley
G. Robinson
Angusine Macgregor
Edward Osmond
John Leigh-Pemberton
Septimus Scott
B. Knight
Ronald Jackson
Clive Uptton
Joan Kiddell-Monroe
David Palmer
Charles F. Tunnicliffe
June Jackson
John Dyke
Mario Capaldi
A.N. Buchanan
Evelyn Bowmar

THE AUTHORS would like to record their gratitude and offer their apologies to the many Ladybird artists whose luminous work formed the glorious wallpaper of countless childhoods. Revisiting it for these books as grown-ups has been a privilege.

Acknowledgements

From the off (10.56am on 25th March 2015, fact fans) a great many people have helped and supported the *Ladybird Books For Grown-Ups* series. (This is sincere, by the way. We've stopped mucking about now. Handbrake turn. This bit's for real.)

First up, our thanks are due to the many Penguinistas who helped the books to life: Dan Bunyard, who enthusiastically took our initial email round the corner to Ladybird and got an instant YES; Ladybird's Creative Director Ronnie Fairweather, the owner of that YES as well as the keys to the Ladybird cupboard, who made everything not just possible but a downright pleasure; Rowland White, our long-suffering editor at Michael Joseph, who published our first book in 2002 and yet still hasn't learned his lesson; his assistants Huw Armstrong, Viola Hayden and Ariel Pakier, who remained calm in the blowback of our many panics; Louise Moore, MD of MJ, who could never be lovelier or more sagacious than she always is; Tom Weldon, CEO of Penguin Random House, who pulled several significant high-profile strings behind the scenes; and our constant travel companion and all-round superpublicist, Ellie Hughes, with whom we've had many memorable encounters, such as the time we shared a Salford tram carriage with a man stone-facedly watching deafening pornography on his phone. Travel broadens the mind.

We've made some walloping friends along the way. Helen Day, Professor of Ladybird at the University of Ladybirdland, has been an amazing help; and, along with the forever-young Jenny Pearce, has nourished us with titbits and kept our spirits up when things have gone wonky. Jenny is one of Douglas Keen's daughters, and we're beyond delighted to know her and her sister, Caroline Alexander. Douglas Keen was the fabulous and brilliant spirit who ran Ladybird for four decades, and his influence can be felt on every page of the original books. We salute him with total reverence.

Our agent of nearly two decades, Cat Ledger, has been a vicious negotiator and steadfast cleverclogs, and we send her reams of thanks (of which she keeps ten per cent).

A few pals have kindly acted in a casual consultancy manner (in other words, we take them down the pub and ask them whether students smell or how it feels to feel *anything whatsoever* about football), and a gratitude-shaped muffin goes to each: Paul Rossi, Ed Morrish, Carrie Quinlan, Mark Evans, Will Maclean and Ian Dunt.

Similarly, Abigail Burdess and Katy Brand were the first readers of *How It Works: The Wife* and we could not have been more grateful for their insight as well as their insistence that we needed to tackle the subject with our studs up (whatever that means).

Our partners, Sue Knowles and Julia Raeside, have put up with a biblical plague of Ladybird books piling up around our homes for years, and (more testingly) have put up with us for years, so they both deserve a fucking medal – as do our kids, Egbert, Volkswagen and Octor Doctopus (not their real names), who are really very good about having dads with such a silly job.

Several of the illustrators' families and models have come forward with smiles on their faces and, since we've been at pains to credit the original artists since day one, it would seem perverse not to mention them here, so thanks are paintballed in the direction of Nick Aitchison, Jane Barnes and Andrew and Jean Glendinning (aka Peter and Jane).

And, for general cheerleading and stuff beyond the call, we must say grats molto to Hattie Adam-Smith, Jesse Armstrong, Richard Ayoade, Sam Bain, Louis Barfe, Nick Barron, Geoff Barrow, Guy Baxter, Kate Bottley, Charlie Brooker, Heather Crossley, Shannon Cullen, Richard Curtis, Steve Doherty, Tim Dunn, Kevin Eldon, Elissa Gay, Bryony Gordon, John Grindrod, Kate Haldane, Rob Halstead, David Headley, Alexandra Heminsley, Tom Hodgkinson, Tom Jackson, Manda Levin, Tim Lewis, Jake Lingwood, Jessie Lowe, Stuart Maconie, Fiona Magee, Lucy Mangan, Simon Mayo, Natasha McEnroe, Andy Miller, David Mitchell, John Mitchinson, Caitlin Moran, Alex Morris, Stuart Murdoch, Sharon O'Dea, Giulio Olivotto, Rosa Olivotto, Clare Parker, Pete Pawsey, Clare Plascow, Robert Popper, David Quantick, Stu Richards, Rowland Rivron, Diedrich Santer, Sarah Scarlett, Imogen Scott, Dan Schreiber, Idil Sukan, Sue Swift, Natt Tapley, Olivia Thomas, Richard Thomas, Damian Treece, David Tyler, Annie Underwood, Jo Unwin, Robert Webb, Josh Weinstein, Séverine Weiss, Judith Woods and everyone who invited us to a literary festival or looked after us while we were there. You all helped, and there is no finer undertaking than helping.

If you bought a book (and, if you didn't, it's hella weird that you're starting here) – thank you. Yes, YOU. Every photo we were sent of someone giggling at a book in a shop – every mention on social media – every 'this was my dad on Christmas Day' picture – even when the books made an appearance on *University Challenge* and *Antiques Roadshow* (both of which happened) – all of it was down to the readers. So thank you all.

We're done here. That's it. Na zdrowie, l'chaim, cin cin and up yer bum.